ANGER
MANAGEMENT

A Professional Guide for **Group Therapy and Self-Help**

MARC NOBLITT, Ph.D. and
JEFFREY CHARLES BRUTEYN, Ph.D.

iUniverse®

ANGER MANAGEMENT
A PROFESSIONAL GUIDE FOR GROUP THERAPY AND SELF-HELP

iUniverse books may be ordered through booksellers or by contacting:

iUniverse
1663 Liberty Drive
Bloomington, IN 47403
www.iuniverse.com
1-800-Authors (1-800-288-4677)

Because of the dynamic nature of the Internet, any web addresses or links contained in this book may have changed since publication and may no longer be valid. The views expressed in this work are solely those of the author and do not necessarily reflect the views of the publisher, and the publisher hereby disclaims any responsibility for them.

Any people depicted in stock imagery provided by Getty Images are models, and such images are being used for illustrative purposes only.
Certain stock imagery © Getty Images.

ISBN: 978-1-5320-6033-5 (sc)
ISBN: 978-1-5320-6034-2 (e)

Library of Congress Control Number: 2018913284

Print information available on the last page.

iUniverse rev. date: 01/22/2019

Contents

Acknowledgements

We would like to thank the following people for all of their help, dedication, and hard work.

A heartfelt thanks goes to Mrs. Lois Whitcraft for providing so much research, advice, and many editing suggestions. From the inception to the completion of this project, you were an inspiration and a great help. To Brian Noblitt, thank you for all of your hard work. Despite numerous other commitments, you tirelessly provided assistance with anything that was needed to bring this project to completion. We would also like to thank Carla Cilvik for editing this work. Your sharp mind and attention to detail helped us make this work clearer in both its presentation and delivery.

To the many people who have provided inspiration and guidance, your contributions made this work what it is. Thank you so much for all of your help. To all those mentioned and unmentioned, please accept our heartfelt appreciation.

-the authors

Introduction

Yep, this is another anger management book. Before you throw it down, ask yourself, "Why another one?" The answer, in part, can be found in baboons.

There is a troop of baboons in eastern Africa. Actually, there is more than one, but this particular troop had a unique anger management transformation. For those of you not familiar with baboons, suffice it to say when the higher ranking (dominant) males get angry, they take it out on the rest of the troop. One season a garbage pile was left with a lot of tainted meat. The dominant males insisted on eating first. This resulted in a massive death of all the angry, high ranking baboons.[1]

After the group funeral for the angry guys, the remainder of the males were easier going, nicer fellows. The whole mood of the troop shifted to calmer and more cooperative. When new, angry adolescents from other troops joined the calm group, within six months they were nicer guys too, with less fighting, less attacking, more cooperation. So how is it a troop of baboons can learn not only to manage their anger, but to teach other baboons as well? The answer does not lie in becoming a baboon or feeding angry people tainted meat. People need to be taught the skills necessary to effectively manage their anger.

Let's assume most of us are as smart, or smarter than a baboon. Baboons don't have short and long-term anger strategies. They do not sit on a couch and role-play their various anger triggers. Yet they can develop social skills that make them less aggressive or angry. For our program we needed to identify:

- What are these skills that we as humans need to learn?
- How can they be structured into our program?

The next ingredient was finding the right audience (the baboons wouldn't sit still) to test the program. For this we worked with inmates in the federal prison system. Trust us when we tell you, failure was not an option. Most anger management programs deal with rage, violent outbursts, and the need for control. Yes, these need to be addressed, but this is not the only expression of unhealthy anger.

Ron and Patricia Potter-Efron, authors and psychologists, are experienced anger management professionals. The importance of their work is recognizing that unhealthy anger can take many forms. Some psychologists, ourselves included, agree with their conclusion that therapy should be adapted to the presenting anger style. Though psychology has long recognized that anger can be expressed with multiple styles, their work lays out a more detailed theory for categorizing it. Passive-aggressive and shame-based anger are examples of different styles. While we believe the chronic anger styles articulated by Ron and Patricia may simply be characteristics of anger, the ability to look at these various anger styles can assist with developing skill training in order to address them more effectively.

Traditional anger management programs either discuss how to be (i.e. more optimistic, less reactive, etc.) or they completely ignore other elements, such as morals, ethics, and the spiritual. In the 1980s medical doctor and psychiatrist Victor Frankl, developed the psychological therapy model of logotherapy. He argued that some problems could not be successfully treated unless people took into account the meaning and purpose in their lives. He also touched on issues of ethics. Many psychologists before him mentioned the importance of looking at issues of morals and ethics, including Freud, Carl Rogers, and Carl Jung. Early in his career Freud postulated that people who lived by strong morals and ethics carried fewer regrets throughout life, and subsequently lived happier, healthier lives. So why did their students and their students' students fail to create programs that included these important points? Following the advice of these former masters, we have incorporated morals into each anger management session.

Originally in designing this program it was predominately intended for professionals who were running their own anger management programs. In applying this program in our classes we have come to find that almost anyone who follows the instructions and weekly exercises receives the benefits of controlling their anger. Aside from professionals, if you are person dealing with anger and are looking for a comprehensive way to treat it, this program can be of immense benefit to you. Simply read each chapter in its entirety, then follow the exercises outlined for that chapter.

The exercises from each chapter are intended to be applied over the course of a week. Though if you are working the program without the help of a counselor you can take longer. Read everything carefully, taking the time to thoroughly learn the material and apply it into your everyday life. If you do that, you can begin getting positive results from the very first session.

For people who might pose a danger to themselves or others, it is necessary that they receive treatment under the supervision of a qualified professional. If you are using this program for yourself, be sure to fully inform your mental healthcare provider.

Often times when psychologists are faced with difficult individuals, medication comes into play. Its most effective role has been demonstrated in the management of severe symptoms in conjunction with therapy and behavioral strategies. The need to treat the entire person, with most of the individual functioning, instead of medicating most of the individual and treating the small part left unimpaired by side effects, is the main concern. Comprehensive treatment plans provide people with tools to help them live better. They are not just about a symptom, diagnosis, or a disorder. They are about the person having a better quality of life. This program considers the treatment of the whole person, the mind, body, and spirit, in effectively managing anger. Its design calls for 12 sessions taught over an equal number of weeks, but applied over a lifetime. Because this program is comprehensive, it can work synergistically with the responsible use of anger related medications.

In designing this program, we realized there are many other missing components in supposed "comprehensive" anger management programs. There are literally years of studies explaining how music, exercises such as yoga, and breathing techniques can assist with calming. When a stressful situation appears, these techniques help to relax the person and generally assist them in maintaining a healthy perspective. Another factor in determining how you handle stress is your nutrition. Your nutrition can literally pump you up or bring you down. The right nutrition keeps you healthy and helps regulate your mood. We also incorporated positive affirmations and positive language. All of these things combined help make you happier, and happy people are less tense and respond to anger better. The final component involves preparing participants for the real possibility of slipping up/back sliding, and how to address it.

These are the components of the program that make it unique. We then identified some of the core skills people need to carry with them into the real world. This is where we turned to positive psychology. It identifies virtues and strengths that happier people tend to have, incorporating them into a theory of psychology. From these strengths, we identified five that are critical in the management of anger. In order to teach them, we had to break them down into component skills. Step by step these can be learned and developed.

In a sense, this is what our baboon troop is doing. They communicate daily which behaviors work and which are being shunned. They never stop their skill development. In our program we develop the following Virtue/Strength/Skills (VSS):

- Optimism
- Self-forgiveness
- Self-control
- Empathy
- Forgiveness of Others

The program includes both short and long-term anger management strategies that include these positive skills. They are versatile strategies applicable to a wide range of real life situations. They are not the rote responses that many other programs suggest. We also include ongoing VSS development exercises, designed to continue your training in these skills. All of these parts combine into a truly comprehensive anger management program that works.

This book is not about the philosophy of what you should do, but how to do it. Most anger management books are long on theory and short on application. After six months, you get some results. But as soon as you leave the troop, you are back to scratching and fighting. You get results while in the program, but then they don't last. This program introduces some theory, but only in respect to developing the needed skills. You take these skills with you. This means you will have the tools you need to deal with anger situations in the real world.

Chapter 1

Positive Psychology

"As a single footstep will not make a path on the earth, so a single thought will not make a pathway in the mind. To make a deep physical path, we walk again and again. To make a deep mental path, we must think over and over the kind of thoughts we wish to dominate our lives." - Henry David Thoreau

It is with light hearted chagrin that we admit taking our first college psychology classes back in the 1980s. Positive psychology had yet to evolve. And when it emerged in the early 1990's, we realized that we were already implementing many of its principles; positive psychology focuses on such things as positive thoughts and actions. Its basic tenets and practices created incredible synergy with our anger management program.

Dr. Martin Seligman wrote, "Before World War II, psychology had three distinct missions: curing mental illness, making lives of all people more productive and fulfilling, and identifying and nurturing high talent". [2] Shortly after WWII, the primary focus of psychology shifted to the first priority, treating abnormal behaviors and mental illness. During the 1950s, humanist thinkers such as Carl Rogers, Erich Fromm, and Abraham Maslow, helped renew interest in other areas by developing theories that focused on happiness and the positive aspects of human nature. [3]

Founded on a focus of helping people prosper and lead healthy, happy lives, Martin Seligman and Mihaly Csikszentmihalyi describe positive psychology as follows: "We believe that a psychology of positive human functioning will arise that achieves a scientific understanding and effective interventions to build thriving in individuals, families, and communities." [4]

Positive Psychology

Seligman postulates that people have a pre-set range for happiness. Just like physical attributes such as body weight, it is largely attributable to genetics. His research shows that this range can be lastingly increased. This task is attempted by focusing on positive psychology's three pillars:

1) The study of positive emotion.
2) The study of positive traits. Traits are defined as virtues, strengths, and abilities. Each of the six virtues are a broad category, with the subcategories being called strengths.
3) The study of positive institutions, such as democracy and strong families.

In terms of the practical application of positive psychology to therapeutic settings, we have applied it regarding the following three points:

1) By improving the positive perception and developing the virtue/strength skills of the individual, they will experience fewer episodes of negative behaviors, such as anger, depression, etc.
2) With appropriate strength development (i.e. optimism and self-control) through developing associated skills, individuals can manage their existing issues, such as anger. Selecting the appropriate strength based skills can help in successfully applying short and long-term behavioral modification strategies.
3) People developing strength related skills are likely to be happier. Happy people are less likely to succumb to anger.

Over the last ten years or so, general interest in positive psychology has grown tremendously. Interest on the topic has also increased on college campuses. Harvard's course on positive psychology became the university's most popular class.[5] Many universities have added PhD programs in this growing field. In order to get a better understanding, let us take a look at positive psychology's history, major theories, and applications.

In 2002 the first international conference on positive psychology was held, and in 2009 the first World Congress on positive psychology took place in Philadelphia. The International Positive Psychology Association (IPPA) has recently been established with thousands of members in over 80 countries with the stated goal of promoting the field of positive psychology. Research from this branch of psychology has seen various practical applications.

The Declaration of Independence states that people are endowed with certain unalienable rights to life, liberty, and the pursuit of happiness, not the right to happiness. One must pursue it. Positive psychology provides a systematic study on how to go about pursuing and sustaining it. In his book "Authentic Happiness ", Martin Seligman, Ph.D. gives a rigorous explanation about what the field of positive psychology identifies as the components of happiness. In his entire work he gives one formula. A person's Happiness Level (H) = S + C + V.[6]

S = Set Range of one's happiness, which is essentially one's happiness thermostat. As a result of studies dealing with identical twins raised apart and adopted children raised in the same household, it is believed that S is attributable to genetics.[7] It accounts for roughly half of a person's score on an enduring happiness test. S also sets the upper limit of a person's happiness. One of the goals of positive psychology is to help people to find ways to live within the upper range of their happiness limit.

C = Circumstances of your life. The most important circumstances of your life regarding happiness are the following: Having a healthy marriage, an active social life, living in a wealthy democracy, being optimistic about your health, and being religious. It is important to note that Dr. Seligman's work identifies the circumstances to avoid are: staying single, divorcing, living under a dictatorship, severe illness, not having a social support system such as from a church or a synagogue, experiencing high levels of negative emotion, being socially isolated, and extreme poverty. Except in unusual cases, the circumstances of your life account from between 8 to 15 percent of your happiness score. It is also important to note that pursuing wealth, just for its own sake, is unlikely to improve your happiness.

If you wanted to raise the C part of the equation as high as possible, you would do the following things:[8]

- Live within or move to a country that is a wealthy democracy.
- Get married (we recommend an emotionally supportive and loving marriage).
- Build a rich social network.
- Actively participate in a positive group. Examples include religion, churches or altruistic organizations.

V = Voluntary Variables. They account for about 40 percent of your score on an enduring happiness test. Because of the variance in genetics and the variance in who experiences the most extreme life circumstances, this number can only be approximated. That 40 percent comes from things directly under your control that can help you live within the upper most range of your potential happiness. Though it is recommended that people improve the circumstances of their life that they are able to change, this course predominately focuses on the V of the happiness formula. In this regard we will discuss the positive psychology subjects of flow, gratification, and virtues/strengths. These things build and sustain positive emotions. They help to make us healthier, more productive, and happier.

According to positive psychologist Mihaly Csikszentmihalyi, flow is a state of being fully engaged. The activity must be challenging enough to require concentration, but not so hard that success is unobtainable. In Mihaly's own words, "The ego falls away. Time flies. Every action, movement, and thought follows inevitably from the previous one, like playing jazz. Your whole being is involved, and you're using your skills to the upmost."[9] Examples of this might include activities such as expressions of art, playing an instrument, writing poetry, playing challenging video games, or any fun activity requiring full concentration.

People usually equate pleasure and gratification, claiming both produce happiness. In positive psychology there is a distinct difference. Pleasure does not produce lasting happiness; gratification does. It was Aristotle who wrote about the difference between bodily pleasures and eudaimonia (happiness). It is from this definition of happiness that positive psychology means "gratification". One person thus explained it, "Pleasure is eating a cake; gratification is having baked that cake yourself".

Gratification is only accomplished by enacting one or more of the six virtues and corresponding 24 strengths (which are discussed below). When you donate time at a homeless shelter, you enact virtues such as humanity or love and transcendence. The enacting of these virtues and corresponding strengths, leave a pleasurable feeling in your wake. That feeling is gratification. Creating gratification requires putting forth effort and using your skills. These skills must be met against challenges commensurate to your own skill level, thus offering the possibility of failure.

While psychology may have tended to ignore the six positive virtues, the fields of philosophy and religion have not. There is an astonishing convergence across many diverse cultures over millennia regarding virtue. The philosophies of Confucius, those of Aristotle and St. Thomas Aquinas, the Bushido samurai code, the Bhagavad-Gita, even the Boy Scouts, as well as other venerable traditions disagree on the details, but all of these codes or philosophies include six core virtues. These are wisdom/knowledge, courage, humanity, justice, temperance, and transcendence.

These ubiquitous virtues exemplify the following 24 underlying strengths:[10]

Wisdom and Knowledge

1. Curiosity/Interest in the World
2. Love of Learning
3. Judgment/Critical Thinking/Open-Mindedness
4. Ingenuity/Originality/Practical Intelligence/Street Smarts
5. Social Intelligence/Personal Intelligence/Emotional Intelligence
6. Perspective

Courage

1. Valor and Bravery
2. Perseverance/Industry/Diligence
3. Integrity/Genuineness/Honesty

Humanity and Love

1. Kindness and Generosity
2. Lovingness and Allowing Oneself to be Loved

Justice

1. Citizenship/Duty/Teamwork/Loyalty
2. Fairness and Equity
3. Leadership

Temperance

1. Self-control
2. Prudence/Discretion/Caution
3. Humility and Modesty

Positive Psychology

Transcendence

1. Appreciation of Beauty and Excellence
2. Gratitude
3. Hope/Optimism/Future-mindedness
4. Spirituality/Sense of Purpose/Faith/Religiousness
5. Forgiveness and Mercy
6. Humor
7. Zest/Passion/Enthusiasm

Each of the six virtues can be developed through their corresponding strengths. Each of these strengths can be developed through corresponding skill sets, which can be learned. Individually, each of these strengths provide people a number of benefits across a wide spectrum of areas, such as happiness, health, and social benefits. We are one of the first to take strengths and develop them through a series of skill training exercises. We accomplished this by identifying the base skills that lead to the development of these virtues/strengths. We also take an initial measurement of the acquisition of these skills. We refer to these combined virtues/strengths/skills as VSS. The development of these strengths was then applied in a therapeutic manner to anger management. In this context we chose to develop four strengths: optimism, self-control, kindness (empathy), and forgiveness (both of self and others).

Optimism skills counteract negative thinking, help you to anticipate positive outcomes, provide motivation during back-sliding, help pessimists gain balanced perspective, and directly apply to some anger styles and nearly all negative situations. Optimism is shown by numerous studies to improve quality of life in a broad number of ways.[11] Optimism is one of the first skills we develop during the 12 session program. The optimism base skill is how to derive positives as counter arguments to negative observations. The optimism skill sets we designed are invaluable in proactively avoiding anger situations and reducing the residual emotions of anger episodes.

Self-control is relevant to every anger style, short and long-term strategy, and is needed for Behavioral Modification Strategies. People tend to ignore the many acts of self-control they exhibit. A person who generally drinks two cups of coffee per day, who then chooses to drink only one cup for a few days, has shown self-control. The challenge in developing self-control is to assign people achievable tasks and ensure they are aware of their successes. The base skills of self-control are the ability to deny a need or behavior and to recognize that self-control is obtainable. We will use task and reward combined with recognition, to the act of self-control. With some anger styles we encourage members listening to others when they are angry. The act of stopping, and listening is a demonstration of self-control, and members should recognize it as such.

Kindness has the acknowledgement of other people's worth at its core. One of the main components of this strength is empathy. It involves discerning and understanding the thoughts, feelings, and viewpoints of others. At its core, it acknowledges others' worth. Developing empathy helps one gain perspective, helps counteract hostile and aggressive thinking toward others, is an intricate part of active listening, and reduces the impact of nearly every anger style. It is also a component in building happiness. Happy people display more empathy. They give more money to strangers, and are more likely to help others than sad people.[12] In this program empathy is developed by recognizing physical emotional cues, as well as examining the ability to accurately assign emotions. Additionally, real life applications are used to perfect this skill set.

Self-forgiveness is taught in session 4 and is the foundation skill set for general forgiveness. Self-forgiveness is a key building block for forgiving others and helping yourself to recognize the benefits of forgiveness. Forgiveness is taught in sessions 10-12, primarily dealing with someone who actually harmed you. Perceived harm, where a person assigns blame to an individual who neither harmed nor intended harm, is not addressed in this course.

Forgiveness is defined by positive psychologist Robert Enright as, "a willingness to abandon one's right to resentment, negative judgment, and indifferent behavior toward one who unjustly hurt us, while fostering the undeserved qualities of compassion, generosity, and even love toward him or her."[13] We concur with him and other experts that it is both a choice and a trained skill, the capacity of which is an intrinsic part of our nature. Forgiveness skills are built by understanding other people's emotions and associating with them the unhealthy effects of non-forgiveness. Forgiveness benefits the one forgiving and creates emotional room for balanced thinking and allows one to let go of past negative feelings. It helps with any anger style where there is a perceived wrong. For individuals who hurt others psychologically or physically, through their anger, asking for genuine forgiveness from those hurt permits us to forgive ourselves. Self-forgiveness adds to the ability to forgive. By developing the skills related to perspective and assignment of blame, guilt is replaced with balanced assessment.

Positive Psychology

Forgiveness also incorporates empathy, helping one to take other's feelings into consideration and perspective. Empathy is an invaluable skill when offering forgiveness to others that "moderately" harmed you. The belief that forgiveness will benefit both the forgiver and the one forgiven, is also a healthy demonstration of optimism. The term moderate is used, because traumatic harm (such as great harm to a family member) tends to create strong emotions, such as hate. In such instances, the strong emotions are best transferred onto an outside source, such as a judicial system.

By developing these particular VSS, and by applying the short and long-term anger strategies taught in the sessions, the strength of perspective is also developed. This combined application of positive psychology not only helps with anger management, but improves other areas of life, helps one experience gratification, and potentially leads to greater happiness.

Chapter 2

Components

There are components we know are necessary in managing anger, and we are not going to ignore them. Many other quality books talk about, but do not explain how to use these components. How many books tell you things like "Forgiveness will help you", without actually teaching you how to effectively do it? We teach you step by step skills. The multiple anger styles and the Positive Psychology skill development exercises drive this program and make it unique. We have also blended six therapeutic components that combine to create something powerful, synergistic, and effective. But enough with the philosophy, let's get to mechanics:

1. Diaphragmatic Breathing
2. Morals Therapy
3. Use of Positive Thoughts and Words
4. Yoga and Physical Exercise
5. Music Therapy
6. Nutrition Recommendations

Each of these components is explained in this chapter. Whenever they are first encountered in the 12 session program, they are explained in sufficient detail for the members. Furthermore, these components have printable handouts found in the appropriate appendices. Each of the appendices also contain further information and/or scientific references for those who are interested.

Components

1. Diaphragmatic Breathing:

Many of our short-term strategies (STS) in response to anger episodes recommend calming. One crucial action that assists in this is breathing. Breathing can directly affect both our sympathetic and parasympathetic nervous system. This means it can both excite us and calm us down. Proper breath control is an extremely important anger management tool. During every session, participants are taken through a diaphragmatic breathing exercise for about 3 to 4 minutes. It is expected that participants will get sufficient practice with this one breathing technique to be able to apply it to the relevant STS and long-term strategies (LTS) throughout the program. The breathing is first performed in session II. The instructions are located there, as well as in appendix Y where they may be printed or electronically sent to participants. For those interested in further reading, appendix Y also contains additional information on breathing as well as scientific references explaining its importance relevant to anger management.

2. Morals Therapy:

From the original conception of this book we knew morals needed inclusion. Morals are not the domain of any one religion. Interestingly, across diverse religions, cultures, and societies, many of the same morals are repeatedly espoused. In the first session we give an example of similar teachings across twelve separate religions. This similarity is probably not coincidence.

Scholars and sages have long taught that there are consequences for our actions. This may be "reaping what you sow", karma, social consequences or legal justice. Even people without moral codes have to follow some rules in society in order to get along. We also believe that if you follow generally agreed upon moral guidelines, you will have less confrontations, less stress, and be happier. If you are not harming others, people are less likely to harm you. You are less likely to cause anger episodes or to involve yourself in them. All of this works well in conjunction with anger management.

In every session, after the LTS, there is a section on moral values. In each case they were chosen because they have some applicability to the anger style(s) discussed in that particular session. If you can truly embrace those values, they will help with some of the anger situations you will face. Throughout the sessions we quote religious books where they teach these same values. Our quotes are by no means an exhaustive list. The majority of the quotes are derived from the Christian Bible. The point is repeatedly made that the exact same moral values can be found in many other religions as well. For those interested in further philosophical reading in regards to morals, we have included additional information in appendix S.

3. Positive Thoughts and Words:

There are numerous studies that support the hypothesis that positive thoughts and words create a healthier person both physically and emotionally. "Change your thoughts and you change your world" - Norman Vincent Peale. This quote, like so many, suggests that positive thoughts can create positive outcomes.

This program recognizes and addresses not only the need for positive thoughts, but positive words. Research suggests that people who use aggressive words, such as cursing, are more susceptible to volatile situations than people whose speech primarily focuses on the positive. Among therapists it is commonly agreed that people with anger issues will express that anger through words. The use of curse words, or words that evoke strong emotional reactions, heightens emotionally charged situations. The challenge the program addresses is how to teach people the skill of positive thinking and expressing it through language. To that end we have incorporated skill training in optimistic thinking as a series of cognitive exercises. This is combined with written expressions of those positive thoughts through counter arguments to the negative thoughts of the participants.

When possible, we have also taken care to present all of the information in a positive way. For instance, the initial 45 question anger probe is always kept in context, avoiding labeling anyone negatively while still working as an indicator. We also keep the STS and LTS focused on positive actions and proactive changes. We set goals on positive outcomes. Things like "back chaining" (in session I) do not focus on failure but direct attention to the point of highest function. These things actively, yet subtly, model to the participants to emphasize the positive.

In each of the sessions we include a positive affirmation. This is intended to be copied or printed and placed in a place where it will be seen daily. Members should read it a few times each day. For instance it could be placed onto a screen saver, cell phone, or a billfold. Each affirmation corresponds to the anger style(s) discussed in that particular session. If members do not have a particular style they generally use, they may use the General Anger Affirmation found in the first session.

Additional information on the philosophy of positive thinking and speech can be found in appendix P.

Components

4. Yoga and Physical Fitness:

It has been demonstrated that exercise is a good physical solution for working out stress, including stress induced by anger. If it is possible, you should exercise regularly in order to regulate your mental, emotional, and physical health. Doctors vary in their recommendations of how much exercise is enough. The benefits of exercise, like anything else, are based on what you put into it. This is also true of yoga. A regular exercise regimen has a wide range of long-term benefits. Generally speaking, 5 to 6 days a week with an hour a day is a good suggestion. Unfortunately this advice is not reasonable for a lot of people. In many situations going into a fitness center and jogging a couple of miles is not practical either. Yoga, and its constituent parts such as breathing and meditation, can be practiced almost anywhere and adjusted to the time-frame you have available. It is also an effective calming strategy in a broad range of environments.

During each session, participants go through a series of "at the desk" yoga stretches that include diaphragmatic breathing. By performing these exercises at the end of every session, it is intended to make the behaviors second nature to the participants. This routine assists with adjusting anger behaviors and mitigating negative reactions to anger situations. These various yoga positions can provide stretching and calming even while a person is seated at a desk or safely stopped in a car. It is recommended that participants explore taking yoga classes outside of the therapy sessions. Additional reading regarding the details of yoga's many benefits are located in appendix Y.

5. Music Therapy:

Music has been shown to affect everything from water crystal formations, plant growth, to animals, and most certainly people. It has been demonstrated that many aspects of music, such as the lyrics, beat, and loudness can affect mood and emotion. There are several genres of music which have calming effects on the emotions of the listener.

The lyrics and musical combinations can add to the efficacy of techniques you might use to calm yourself. This also leads to a more effective mental state. This in turn permits you to consider the perspective of the situation and focus on resolution. Music that promotes positive mental states is also conducive to the breathing and stretching exercises practiced in the sessions.

By using positive music with breathing and seated stretching exercises, participants experience the benefits first hand. This demonstrates that the combination of breathing, yogic stretching, and music is attainable in environments such as the home, work, or an unmoving car, and is easily accessible to everyone.

When selecting music for the sessions, choose it using the following criteria:

- Only use music with positive lyrics and themes, or no lyrics.
- Choose slow to moderate music, around 60 beats per minute. Slower music brings the heartbeat more in line with the speed of the music, calming you down.
- Absolutely no angry, tense or aggressive music. The following music and genres all have songs that fit this criteria:

Jazz, Classical, Religious Music, Opera, Nature Sounds, Meditation Music, Love Songs, Hymns, Chants, Cultural such as Native or Aboriginal, Soft Rock, Easy Listening and instrumental such as Mandolin, Harp, or Flute.

Music therapy is first discussed in session II. A music handout may be printed from appendix M and given (or electronically sent) to the members. For those interested in the details of positive music, negative music, and supporting scientific references, they may refer to appendix M for further reading.

6. Nutrition:

Almost every psychologist knows that poor nutrition can affect your mood. Likewise, good nutrition can enhance your body, mind and emotions in many ways. Despite this knowledge most programs fail to make ANY mention of it. If you had a room full of people dealing with anger issues, would you really feed them lots of donuts (sugar), caffeine, and salty snack foods and not expect it to make their mood worse? Part of the reason people do this is because in moderation these things make you feel good. But if they are a major part of your daily diet (and for many people they are), they are doing the opposite. They are adding to depression and anxiety, probably making you more sensitive to the things that bother you (Triggers).

There are schools that have radically reduced the incidence of behavior issues in the children simply by only providing them with healthy meals.[14] This same concept also works for adults. Nutrition is briefly discussed in the very first session, with a handout (or file) given to the members at that time. The handout, along with additional nutritional information and scientific references, is located in appendix N. Participants interested in further reading, beyond the handout, should refer to that appendix.

Chapter 3

Session I: Generalized Anger

"Every day we have plenty of opportunities to get angry, stressed, or offended. But what you're doing when you indulge these negative emotions is giving something outside yourself power over your happiness. You can choose to not let little things upset you." - Joel Osteen

If you are running an anger management group, you may follow the session chapters exactly as written, making modifications based on your group size, the time you have allotted, and your personal experience. For the purpose of this work we will use the terms "Counselor" and "Group Leader" interchangeably. Members, Group Members, and Participants are also used interchangeably.

1. Session Overview:

- Anger Myths
- Group Rules and in-group timeout
- Antecedent Behaviors, Triggers, Cues, Anger Invitations
- Anger Control Today (ACT) sheet
- Generalized Anger
- Positive Psychology: week 1 Optimism training

2. Handouts:

Provide members with relevant handouts for the first session. This may include:

- Anger Myths (Appendix G)
- Group Rules (Appendix G)
- 45 Question Anger Styles Test (Appendix G)
- Anger Control Today (ACT) sheet (Appendix A)

3. Anger Myths:

Group leaders should read the following aloud to the group or review it using their own words. It is also located in Appendix G, where it may be printed or electronically dispensed to the members.

Myth #1: Anger is not Inherited.

It is "politically correct" to tell people that anger is solely their fault and within their total control. Several recent studies with identical twins have shown that personality traits, such as anger, may have up to a 50% genetic component.[15] How we behave may be under our control, or can be learned to be controlled.

Myth #2: Anger Always Leads to Aggression.

A similar myth involves the misconception that the only effective way to express anger is through aggression. It is a common misconception that anger builds and escalates to the point of an aggressive outburst. Anger does not need to lead to aggression. Anger management involves incorporating a variety of behavioral strategies and self-assessment techniques to counteract this aggression.

Myth #3: People Must Be Aggressive to Achieve What They Want.

Many times people confuse aggression with assertiveness. To assertively pursue a goal (professional, personal) with a single minded determination can be seen as aggressive. However, the emotion of aggression is a hostile or destructive tendency or behavior.

Session I: Generalized Anger

Myth #4: Venting Anger is Always Desirable.

For many years it has been popular among mental health professionals to allow patients to release their anger in an aggressive manner. Some therapists have implemented the use of beating pillows or punching bags. We acknowledge that this is a component of Progressive Desensitization Therapy, which in the short-term has shown some effectiveness. Consistent with other research, we believe such treatment only becomes effective once the physical and verbal aggression cease. When venting disrupts aggressive mental patterns, such as by taking a walk, it becomes a short-term strategy (STS). When venting reinforces anger patterns through cognitive rehearsal, it is destructive and unhealthy. Research has found that, in the long run, people who vent their anger aggressively simply get better at being angry.[16] Venting anger in an aggressive manner usually just reinforces the aggressive behavior.

Myth #5: If a Person Relapses They Have Failed.

A) Relapse refers to losing control sufficiently to dictate the need to implement a short-term strategy(s). This is a normal occurrence with any behavior that one is trying to change. A person does not fail from relapsing. A person fails by giving up or by failing to continue working on making positive changes. If a relapse should occur, have the patience and endurance to continue the therapy process. This is the time to apply more effort, utilizing back chaining as recommended.

B) Back Sliding and Back Chaining:

Most people will "slip" when they are following a behavioral modification plan. When that happens, it is not a reason to give up on the plan. What the person should do is go back to the point in the plan (Back Chaining) where they were having the most success, and then begin at that point.

4. Basic Instructions to Group Leaders:

Counselors/Group Leaders should start by stating their background and credentials. The Counselor should relate any pertinent background information they may have regarding their own anger management. This sharing should be sufficient to establish authority on the subject, but kept at a minimal amount in order to avoid influencing the group members. In this session the Group Leader provides a basic conceptual framework in a way the group understands. Depending on the ages and backgrounds of the participants, the presentation will vary dramatically. Groups work best when participants become comfortable with one another. We suggest that each participant make a brief introduction explaining why they are there and what they hope to gain from the program. The Counselor should share their goals for the class, which may include the following:

- Help members manage their anger
- Stop violent behaviors or threat making
- Develop self-control over thoughts and actions
- Receive support and feedback from other people in the group
- Learn different skills for empowering long-term management of anger
- Identify each individual's anger styles
- Learn recovery strategies (back-chaining) for relapse
- Learn short-term strategies for dealing with uncontrolled outbursts or initial unhealthy responses to an anger episode

Unlike traditional anger therapy models, these sessions were designed with the idea that one size does not fit all. Some group leaders may be working with more tranquil individuals. Others may be working with historically more violent group members at a correctional or psychiatric facility. After sufficient familiarization with the background material in the introduction and beginning chapters, the group leaders should be able to adapt this program to meet the needs of their specific group. For instance, if group leaders find that there is a predominance of one or more anger styles being presented by the group, the program should be adjusted to meet the specific needs of those members

The program is designed to constitute twelve 90-minute sessions, with a 15 minute break within the session. With breaks, each session would be expected to be about 1 hour and 45 minutes. Except for a few exercises, such as yoga and breathing, we have not suggested the time you take for each section. Based upon the total time you have allotted, the information you want covered, and the level of active participation of your group participants, you may emphasize or deemphasize parts of this comprehensive program. We have included all of the tools we believe you need to help facilitate positive change in your group members. Used in conjunction, these tools make this program much more effective and practical than other anger management models.

An anger management class can be an emotionally charged and intense environment. It is especially important for counselors to develop rapport with each of the participants. Emotionally charged subjects, such as violence, torture, and child abuse should be brought up with care, without directing the discussion toward any one individual. When broaching one of these topics, the counselor should preface with an acknowledgement that it is not directed at anyone in the group, and that the topic may cause some group members emotional discomfort. Due to the potential volatility of these topics, before raising them group leaders should use their counseling experience to gauge the anxiety level of the group. Some of these subjects more naturally lend themselves to later sessions, such as when dealing with the resentment/hate anger style. When rapport and trust levels are high in the class, it is easier for people to learn from the advice of counselors and other participants.

5. Group Rules:

Review with the members the version of the Group Rules used in your sessions. For an example of group rules see the ones we use in Appendix G.

A) Group Safety: No violence or threats toward staff or other participants will be permitted. People only feel comfortable sharing in an environment that is perceived as a sanctuary.
B) Confidentiality: What happens in therapy sessions stays in therapy sessions. Some counselors may have members sign a confidentiality agreement regarding the disclosure of other members personal information.

To the Counselors: It should be noted that mental health professionals are bound to report certain actions or disclosures to the authorities. These actions/disclosures may include physical or sexual abuse inflicted on a child younger than age 18, a person older than 65, or a dependent adult. Reporting abuse of these persons supersedes confidentiality laws involving clients and health professionals. Similarly, if a group member threatens to harm another person, the group leader is required, under the Tarasoff Ruling[17], to warn the intended victim and notify the authorities.

Under reporting requirements, a credible threat has one of the following two criteria:

1) The person has the ability to carry out the threat.
2) The person declares a specific action that could result in harm or death of others.

In the Tarasoff case, the counselor notified the police and warned the victim's mother of the threat. The court ruled this was insufficient since the counselor failed to follow up with police to verify the police had taken action. It is imperative that counselors both notify the proper authorities and parties and follow up with them to ensure that they have acted on the counselor's advice.

C) In-class and Homework Assignments: Brief in-class and homework assignments will be given each week. Homework will consist of compiling a weekly assessment of the anger meter, continuing to update the Anger Control Today (ACT) sheet, and completing the various exercises that occur throughout the sessions. By completing the homework assignments, participants develop and refine individual behavioral management strategies, as well as allow more active participation in the therapy sessions. Homework assignments provide opportunity for development and refinement. Like any type of skill development, anger management requires time and consistent practice in order to create lasting change.

D) Absences and Cancellations: Members must notify the group leaders in advance if they cannot attend a session. Due to the plethora of material and the way the information builds upon itself, members may not miss more than 2 of the 12 sessions. If more than 2 sessions are missed, the participant may still attend the remaining sessions, but a certificate of completion may not be issued. Participants may join another class as space becomes available. Everyone has days they just do not want to show up to something. The group leader should encourage participants to attend every session. Those potentially missed sessions are the very ones that are often the most beneficial.

E) Timeout: Group leaders reserve the right to call for a group timeout. A group timeout is simply defined as terminating or interrupting the discussion. If a group member feels that their anger over a certain person or subject matter is beginning to escalate out of control, then they should request the group leader for a group timeout. Once a group timeout has been called, the entire group will immediately stop discussing the issue that has caused the proposed escalation. If the person whose anger has escalated simply cannot tolerate the group, they may leave the group for a cool down period, usually five or ten minutes. Once the participant feels emotionally ready, they may rejoin the group. If it is possible, such individuals should be considered for individual counseling to determine a plan of action for dealing with the triggering event. In session V, timeouts are discussed in more detail using the LEAP method, which is a self-directed timeout. It is hoped that after session V, group participants will be able to call an individual timeout for themselves, thus we have left the introduction of the LEAP until then. It is also important to make sure that members do not use any timeout as a therapy avoidance technique.

Session I: Generalized Anger

6. Anger Style Probe:

Anger is generally expressed as either inward anger or explosive anger. It is categorized as inward (masked anger), explosive anger, and chronic anger. It can be further subdivided into various anger styles. For the purposes of this course, we have chosen the eleven most prevalent, together with an accompanying anger probe found in the book *Letting Go Of Anger* by Dr. Efron.[18] We have modified this test and its presentation for the Group Anger Management setting. Ideally, before the first session, each member will have already taken the 45 question Anger Probe found in Appendix G. Understanding each of the Anger Styles can act as a beacon pointing members toward understanding the root causes of their individual anger. The questionnaire is NOT a diagnostic tool. The results are simply an indicator. It is also common for people to exhibit more than one anger type (style). Each of the 11 anger styles are covered in detail in the upcoming sessions. The questionnaire also includes the only biographical intake in the program. All of the future instruments and exercises just ask for the participant's name. This assumes that a separate and organized file is maintained of each participant.

When evaluating the probe, every three questions correlate to one of the 11 anger styles in the following questions:

1-3 Anger Avoidance
4-6 Sneaky Anger / Passive Aggressive
7-9 Anger Turned Inward
10-12 Sudden Anger
13-15 Shame-based Anger
16-18 Deliberate Anger
19-21 Excitatory Anger
22-24 Resentment / Hate
25-27 Habitual Hostility
28-30 Paranoia
31-33 Moral Anger

Questions 34-45 further subdivide Anger Turned Inward. Anger styles rarely present themselves as neatly defined and discreet categories. They often blend together. It is quite probable that a person with Anger Turned Inward exhibits a combination of the following inward patterns, scored as follows:

34-36 Self-blame
37-39 Self-sabotage
40-42 Self-neglect
43-45 Self-attack

Consider the first three questions of the probe:

1) I try never to get angry.
2) I get really nervous when others are angry.
3) I feel I'm doing something bad when I get angry.

A person who answers "yes" on one or two of the above questions exhibits some signs of the anger avoidance anger style. Encourage that person to pay special attention when that anger style is discussed during group therapy. That person may also record it in their ACT sheet. If a person answered "yes" to all three questions, have them record "Anger Avoidance" on their ACT and encourage that person to pay special attention when that anger style is discussed in the upcoming sessions. In the case of questions 34-45, they all deal with some aspect of Anger Turned Inward. There is no objective number of yes's a person must score before one can definitely say they are dealing with a particular sub-category of Anger Turned Inward. Look for patterns in this probe that correlate with other observed behaviors in order to adjust the short and long-term strategies used by members in their Anger Control Today (ACT) plan.

7. Antecedent Behaviors:

These are all the relevant behaviors that led up to the triggering anger event. By themselves these behaviors can be innocuous. In the context of certain environments, triggers, or behavior order, they can elicit an anger response. Because they are part of the anger cycle, they are important to identify and bring to conscious attention with the intent of disrupting that cycle. Examples of potential Antecedent Behaviors are as follows:

- Going to certain locations, such as a particular bar or person's house
- Consciously involving yourself with activities, people, and environments that are likely to trigger your anger.
- Intoxication or Drug Use before an anger episode

Session I: Generalized Anger

8. Anger Triggers:

An Anger Trigger is any stimulus that makes a person generally angry. Nearly anything can act as a trigger for a person. Examples may include:

- People
- Places
- Things
- Statements
- Differing Opinions

9. Anger Cues:

Anger cues are signs that one is becoming angry. They are divided into four categories. Examples include:

1. Physical: sweating, hot flashes, increased heartbeat, tightness in chest, or nervous ticks
2. Emotional: fear, anxiety, annoyance, guilt, jealousy, anger, and for some even excitement
3. Behavioral: raising voice, making a fist, hitting hands together, moving into someone's personal space, pacing, cursing
4. Cognitive: thinking harm of others, thoughts of revenge, negative or hostile self-talk

10. Anger Invitations:

An Anger Invitation is the point when the individual, through strategy or conscious decision, can become angry or choose not to become angry. In part, the decision to react or give into the anger depends on the severity of the Trigger experienced by the individual.

11. Anger Control Today (ACT):

An Anger Control Review is performed in each of the proceeding sessions. Between the sessions members are to answer the questions on their ACT sheets. These observations are emailed to the counselor at least two days before the next session. The ACT sheet six sections, as follows:

1. Anger Meter
2. Type of Anger

3. Anger Triggers
4. Anger Cues
5. Short-term Strategies/STS
6. Long-term Strategies/LTS

<u>Anger Meter</u>: One of the best techniques for managing anger is being able to monitor it. Having an anger meter is an extremely effective method to make a cognitive/emotional assessment of the level of anger one is experiencing in most situations. Imagine a thermometer with a ten at the highest point and one at the lowest point. When a person encounters an anger provoking event, the anger starts at a lower level and then escalates. Between now and the next session, members are to record the highest level of anger attained during the week, and the accompanying questions on the ACT sheet.

Every person's individual anger meter is going to differ. In order to normalize this subjective scale between group members, the following definitions for 1, 3, and 5 are offered:

1 = minimal anger, a level of calmness
3 = This is the tipping point between manageable and potentially uncontrollable behaviors, where short-term strategies are effective. Depending upon the Anger Style(s) of the individual, a 3 may include the following examples:

- Moving into another person's space
- Raising one's voice above a conversational tone
- Blood pressure or heart rate increases

3 to 4 = It is recommended a person use the LEAP method of timeout as discussed in session V.
5 = The highest level of anger a given individual may experience. It may include one or more of the following examples:

- Doing harm to oneself or others
- Preparing for a violent episode
- Continuous screaming of profanity and/or threats

<u>Type of Anger</u>: After an anger episode, answer Y/N for explosive or inward. If a specific style was expressed, record that style here.

Session I: Generalized Anger

<u>Anger Cues</u>: Sample anger cues are listed on the ACT. Check all appropriate cues of the incident with the highest recorded number on the anger meter. Fill in any additional cues not listed.

<u>Anger Triggers</u>: Trigger categories are listed with some space for members to fill in the individual details of that trigger.

<u>Short-Term Strategies</u>: Toward the end of this session some general anger STS and LTS are discussed. In each upcoming session a short-term and a long-term strategy is introduced for the anger style(s) of that given session. On the ACT sheet, members should record any STS used when they obtained their highest number on the anger meter that week.

<u>Long-Term Strategies</u>: Members should record any LTS used as a result of the anger episode.

12. Generalized Anger:

Anger is one of the basic human emotions. Generalized anger is not style specific. It may be inward anger, explosive, or a combination. Anger is generally believed to have both benefits and negative consequences.

13. Anger Benefits:

Discuss the following concepts with the group:

In the short-term, expressing and acting on anger seems to have immediate benefits. Use of anger may allow a person to more easily manipulate others. It may give them a false sense of security, control over others, or control of a situation. Initially the display of anger may seem to reduce tension, allowing a person to feel better.

14. Negative Consequences of Anger:

Ask the class, "What are the possible negative consequences of anger?" Get individual answers and a group opinion. Project (or place) the three categories on the board and fill in the consequences as they are called out, adding what is not called.

A) Health: Increased blood pressure, increased heart rate, hypertension, arteriole sclerosis, weight gain, and decreased immune efficiency which makes one susceptible to illness and disease. Point out that these are all consequences of stress.

B) Violence: Injury, retaliation, loss of life, fired from a job, regret, negative feelings about self, arrest/detention

C) Social: Verbal abuse, intimidation, threatening behavior (others feeling fear), resentment, decreased trust, alienation for/toward aggressor, removal from clubs/groups, missed business opportunities, less financial success, less successful personal relationships, loneliness, poverty or living far below your economic potential.

15. General Anger Short-term Strategies (STS):

Short-term strategies can be immediately implemented when a member is first aware they are becoming angry. They should be utilized in order to prevent an escalation of anger. Examples of this may be taking a walk or performing slow, deep abdominal breathing. The short-term strategies in this session can be used for any anger styles. Throughout the course, the strategies that are style-specific are marked as such. Discuss the following STS with the members.

A) Diaphragmatic Breathing STS: At the end of the remaining sessions, the same abdominal breathing exercise is performed. It is intended for members to become proficient with this technique during the 12 sessions. It is explained in detail in part 17 of session II.

B) Timeout STS: Be sure to remove yourself to a lower stress environment. By pausing, one has time to assess the situation and consider options. It "interrupts" the anger response pattern. In session V, the LEAP method of timeout is discussed in more detail.

C) Constructive Communication STS: Focus on calming and invite constructive communication. Begin with listening and then being listened to, without interruption.

16. General Anger Long-term Strategies (LTS):

The following long-term strategies reduce stress or improve coping skills. They are therefore applicable to all anger styles. Some of the LTS enhance specific skills such as perception, self-control and empathy. For instance, the ability for one to be objective and empathic helps mitigate the intensity of dealing with moral anger. All strategies, both short and long-term, only work if people apply and feel comfortable with them. Discuss with the members the following strategies:

A) Implementing Behavioral or Cognitive LTS treatment plans. The individual Anger Styles LTS in the sessions accomplish this.

B) ACT: Applying the ACT sheet.

C) Perspective and Perception skill training LTS: Many of the STS, LTS and some of the VSS skills also incorporate perspective and perception. Perspective and perception are discussed in session II.

D) VSS Training LTS: Continuing positive psychology Virtue/Strength/Skill (VSS) training: self-control, optimism, self-forgiveness, empathy, forgiveness of others. These skills are developed in each of the sessions.

E) Exercise LTS: We suggest 30 minutes per day for 5-6 days per week for the anger management benefits. If you safely exercise for longer periods, the benefits may increase proportionally. Some doctors and exercise specialists recommend more exercise than 30 minutes a day for those who have the capacity, time, and inclination.

17. Generalized Anger Positive Affirmation:

Discussed in the components chapter of this program, a new positive affirmation is presented in each session. Each affirmation is applicable to that session's corresponding anger style. We recommend the affirmation most appropriate for each person be copied and placed where they will regularly see it. This may be on a screen saver, inside a wallet, or taped to a mirror. The affirmation should be read each day, preferably several times per day. It is a continual reminder of the things you wish improved.

I acknowledge that anger is a normal emotion.
Like all emotions, I will only use it in positive ways.
I seek to always do the right thing.
I am transforming into the best person I can be.

18. Moral Values:

In each of the upcoming sessions we discuss moral values pertinent to that particular anger style. We expressed in earlier chapters that morals are not exclusive to any one particular religion, nor is it solely the domain of religion. The moral values we espouse in these sessions are universally accepted by the world's most prevalent religions. We also acknowledge that people without any faith may be moral. Below are some examples of quotes from a dozen religions, showing the universal acceptance morals have. Group leaders need not read every quote to make the point.

- Christianity: Do unto others as you would have them do unto you.
- Judaism: What is hateful to you, do not do to your neighbor. This is the whole Torah, all the rest is commentary.
- Islam: None of you truly have the faith if you do not desire for your brother that which you desire for yourself.
- Hinduism: Do not to others that which if done to you would cause you pain.
- Buddhism: Hurt not others that you yourself would find harmful.
- Wicca: If it harm none, do what you will.
- Zoroastrianism: Do not do unto others all that which is not well for oneself.
- Jainism: In happiness and suffering, in and joy and grief, we should regard all creatures as we regard ourselves.
- Baha'i: Lay not on any soul a load that you would not wish to be laid upon you and desire not for anyone the things you would not desire for yourself.
- Native America: Respect for all life is the foundation.
- Confucianism: Do not do unto others what you do not want others to do unto you.
- Sikhism: Don't create enmity with anyone as God is within everyone.

From a moral viewpoint, anger is to be avoided. If one has an anger problem, they should work on improving it.

- "One must especially strive not to become angered or to be an angry person, for these traits are despicable and they destroy one's life". - Rabbi Moshe Weiner [19]
- In the Islamic Hadith a follower of Muhammad asks three times to be advised. Each time Muhammad responds, "Do not become angry".
- In Buddhism, "Give up anger...Conquer anger with non-anger...Guard against anger erupting in your body...Guard against anger erupting in your speech...Guard against anger erupting in your mind". [20]
- "Be angry, and yet do not sin; do not let the sun go down on your anger" (Ephesians 4:26).

Session I: Generalized Anger

19. Positive Psychology:

Each of the sessions contain Virtue/Strength/Skill (VSS) development exercises. If your program provides for individual therapy, these various positive psychology instruments are beneficial in assessing each individual member's progress, level of participation, and skill in that particular area.

    A) Optimism: week 1/scenario 1

Distribute the Week 1 / In-class Scenario for Optimism. Members should read the scenario, then answer the questions that follow. There are no right or wrong answers. Over the course of the program, completion of these in-class scenarios and out-of-class exercises is essential to the development of the corresponding VSS. At the beginning of session IV, after the completion of all the optimism exercises, there is a debriefing. There, the optimism exercises are further explained and any remaining questions are answered.

    B) Optimism: week 1/out-of-class exercise 1:

Give the members the out-of-class exercise, located in Appendix B. Answer any questions that members may have regarding completion of the assignment.

20. Nutrition:

Not only does nutrition impact our health and well-being, it can affect our moods. There are literally encyclopedias full of current information on proper nutrition. Teaching it is beyond the scope of this course. However, it would be remiss to fail to mention it. Explain that nutrition is important to emotional wellness and those interested in the subject should further educate themselves. Located in appendix N, pass out or send the following handout regarding the basics of nutrition.

1. If possible, predominately eat whole foods such as nuts, grains, fruits, vegetables, fish, cheese, and meat.
2. Avoid the following: processed foods, refined sugar, tobacco, artificial sweeteners, saturated fats, and drugs.
3. Consume in moderation or caution: caffeine, alcohol, and table salt.

4. Follow the restrictions of your doctor, such as those with gout consuming less meat and cheese.

5. Get sufficient sleep. Lack of sleep can cause irritability and negatively affect your health. For most adults sufficient sleep is about 6 to 8 hours per night.

21. Homework:

- Review the rules and regulations
- Use the Anger Control Today (ACT). Members are to answer the six questions regarding the anger episode with the highest number on the scale during the week. Email the observations to the counselor two days prior to the next session.
- Complete the week 1 optimism out-of-class exercise 1.
- Begin using an anger affirmation daily as part of your overall anger management plan.

Chapter 4

Session II: Anger Avoidance

"It is not that I am incapable of anger...(but) there is always in me the conscious struggle for following the law of non-violence deliberately and ceaselessly". - Mahatma Gandhi

1. Update and Review:

   A) Review with members any questions they have regarding the previous session regarding generalized anger. Members should have their Anger Control Today (ACT) files available, updating it when appropriate.
   B) Optimism Week 1/Review:

The in-class scenario gave practice in developing a positive actions list. The out-of-class exercise was intended to expand upon that skill. They were intended to determine how comfortable you are with seeing positive actions, either by yourself or with someone else during a day.

To Counselors: If the out-of-class exercise was not emailed, collect it now. Answer any questions the members may have, filing away any regarding the exercise's psychology until the optimism debriefing in session IV.

   C) Anger Style Probe:

This test was either emailed to the counselor (ideally) before the first session, or completed in the first session. Group leaders should return the results of the anger probe to the members. Remind the group this is not a diagnostic instrument but an indicator. All people have anger and consequently use different styles to express that anger. Most people also exhibit more than one anger style. This probe is used to identify the individual ways members express their anger. It is a starting point for their ACT plan, and is not intended to define or label them. One way to present the class information would be to place the results of the probe on the board, obviously not identifying anyone by name. This way members can see what types of anger styles are involved in the class, and see that their peers are having similar issues with anger. Members should record any anger styles that they use onto their ACT sheet.

2. Anger Control Today (ACT):

Conduct an Anger Control Review. This involves discussing with the members the anger episode where they recorded their highest number on the anger meter. The purpose of the review is the following:

- Familiarize members with using the ACT as an ongoing treatment plan.
- Help members to identify the elements of the ACT, such as cues, triggers, and appropriate strategies.
- It is an opportunity for members to discuss their issues and listen to the issues of others.
- When conducting this review, reinforce the positive solutions and strategies implemented by the members.

3. Session Overview:

- Positive Psychology: Optimism week 2
- Discuss Anger Avoidance
- Morals Therapy
- Yoga Therapy
- Diaphragmatic Breathing

4. Positive Psychology:

Optimism has many benefits. Optimists live long, enjoy more social advantages, have happier marriages, have better health habits, lower blood pressure, and tend to make more pay. Optimism is a core strength in building happiness and is a key component in developing the perspective and objective thinking necessary to counteract many anger styles.

Session II: Anger Avoidance

A) Optimism: week 2/scenario 2:

Give the members the second scenario, located in Appendix B. Now members are asked to list both positive and negative actions in a hypothetical event. Have members read the scenario and answer the proceeding questions.

B) Optimism: week 2/Out of Class Exercise 2:

Give members the out-of-class exercise 2, located in Appendix B. Answer any questions the members may have regarding completing the task. Screen any questions regarding the test's psychology, reserving those for the optimism debriefing in session IV.

The assignment and exercise 2 add some gray elements to the equation. We are now asking everyone to find positive and negatives in the scenario and in out-of-class events which would usually be considered negative. We want to know how easily everyone is able to find the negatives and positives in these types of situations.

5. Anger Avoidance:

Anger avoidance is mostly based on fear. It is the fear of loss of control, consequences, or rejection. It can become a comprehensive coping mechanism, where a person tries avoiding anything they find too emotionally charged or unpleasant. It is sometimes based on the fear of guilt (good people don't get mad). While not suggesting group members follow the Jedi philosophy, there is some validity to the quote from Star Wars Jedi Master Yoda, "Fear leads to anger, anger leads to hatred, hatred leads to the dark side. Once you journey down its path, forever will it dominate your destiny". Some people are just afraid if they allow themselves to feel their anger, they will be stuck in that anger, later regretting their actions. People who use this style of anger may exhibit the following behaviors:

- Show fear toward anger, either their own or others.
- Ignore their own anger, downplaying or denying its existence.
- Feel guilty about feeling their anger.
- Feel uncomfortable when others exhibit signs of anger.
- Feel that anger is socially acceptable.

- Prevent others from expressing or showing their anger without leaving the scene or environment.
- After the situation has ended, participation in self-recrimination for not having acted on their anger.

Anger avoiders feel uncomfortable facing anger, often ignoring it. When forced to confront anger, their stress and anxiety will significantly rise. This tends to reduce their ability to constructively address the situation. Anger avoiders look to escape (leave) or be silent when someone initiates a confrontation. Leaving removes them from the situation. Silence gives the avoider the false sense of control, but usually leads to self-recrimination later. The avoider ruminates on what they should or could have done.

Avoiders may screen information that might make them angry, choosing instead not to hear it. One may know their boss is upset, so they avoid them. One may suspect their spouse has lied to them, but they will never discuss the subject. The avoider will choose not to speak about things that will result in conflict. In more extreme cases, the exhibition of anger by others elicits the avoidance pattern. Example: if two family members are arguing, the avoider may demand the argument cease while the avoider is in the room. The need to suppress all anger situations, even if the argument between the other two parties may be constructive, causes the avoider to be a problematic factor in the group's communication. This may cause the situation to be needlessly protracted.

6. Benefits of Anger Avoidance:

A) In this and all the remaining sessions we list some of the benefits and consequences of each particular anger style. Anger avoidance has some benefits. Anger avoiders:

- Selectively avoid anger invitations and overt conflicts.
- Save mental and emotional energy that would have been channeled into anger.
- Are able to avoid harm and loss from direct conflict.
- Do not risk being ostracized for expressing their anger.
- Have time to consider an appropriate strategy or tool for dealing with the cause of their anger.

Session II: Anger Avoidance

B) Healthy Anger Exercise

Not all anger is detrimental. Healthy people will become angry in a responsible way. Have the members give some examples of healthy anger. Examples may include:

- Anger can be a signal that real problem is occurring.
- Anger can help one to deal with a threat.
- Healthy anger can be expressed without losing control.
- Anger may convey the seriousness of the situation or that one's feelings have been hurt.
- Healthy anger is relinquished when the situation is resolved.
- Healthy anger is almost never harmful or dangerous.

7. Negative Consequences of Anger Avoidance:

Anger avoiders:

- May not get what they really wanted.
- Deny the natural anger within themselves.
- Inaction may cause them to become angry with themselves. This is not meant in terms of venting. People who fail to take action, when they know they should, subject themselves to cognitive dissonance and the resultant stress that imposes.
- May endanger themselves by a lack of assertive responses. Their inaction puts them in danger.
- Risk that the causes of their anger, left unresolved, may grow into an intolerable situation.

8. Perspective and Perception:

It is important to remember that different people can take completely different feelings from the same experience. Give your class a few short examples:

- People generally do not like waiting in lines. For some people, it causes them to become agitated, angry and even aggressive. There are other people who take such an opportunity to read a good book or to have a personal conversation with their date. By tuning into their perception, adjusting their perspective, and adapting their behavior, they take what many consider an unpleasant experience, and turn it into something enjoyable.

- Some people love a lecture on physics.
- Some like opera.
- Some people enjoy prison. Yes, some people actually enjoy it.

Almost every experience can be turned into something positive if looked at and experienced in the right way.

As an example of the power of perspective, pass out the poem titled "Worst Day Ever?" found in Appendix G. It was posted on *PoetryNation* by Chanie Gorkin who described herself as "an 11th grader at an all-girls high school in Brooklyn, NY". The copy of the poem we found was posted by Ronnie Joice on Twitter.[21] This poem clearly demonstrates how the power of Perspective can transform one's experience of a given situation.

9. Creating Win/Win to No Deal Solutions in regard to conflict resolution:

Step 1: Determine if the situation is important enough for confrontation. Is it worth your attention?

Step 2: If yes, invite the other party to talk while one actively listens.

Step 3: After the other party has been fully understood, communicate clearly and politely exactly what you want the end result to be. You should show concern for the other party. By clearly and politely stating the intended outcome, you can diffuse a potential conflict.

Step 4: Be competitive and assertive, but fair. Most synergistic relationships require a Win/Win solution to problems.

Steven Covey explains in his book, *The Seven Habits of Highly Effective People*, the significance of the Win/Win or No Deal philosophy. It is recommended that any group leaders who are not familiar with this material, read the appropriate chapter in Covey's book.[22] He explains six paradigms of human interaction. Each of them have value under certain circumstances. These are most commonly applied in the context of business relationships. The six paradigms are:

1. Win/Lose: I win, you lose. This is the scarcity mentality that says, "I must have everything, there is never enough. I will take from others so that I survive". Comparing

    this to a family meal, it would be where you eat while the rest of the family goes hungry. You are full but the rest of the family build resentment toward you.

2. Lose/Lose: No one wins. Over a disagreement, you might throw the entire dinner away.

3. Lose/Win: You give up. After an argument, you might leave hungry and everyone else eats.

4. Win: This is where you only concern yourself with getting your own needs met. You let the other person worry about whether or not their needs are being met. Regarding the meal, you eat your fill without passing the bowl or concerning yourself over others.

5. Win/Win: Both parties' needs are mostly met. Perhaps you share the meal and trade parts that are each other's favorites. Long-term relationships, both business and personal, only last if both parties mutually benefit. If there is sufficient trust between the parties, the Win/Win exchange can occur over multiple transactions in order to balance the ledger both ways.

6. Win/Win or No Deal: Covey explains you should be willing to walk away from any deal that fails to be a win/win for both parties. This adds the No Deal option. In the long run all relationships only work if all parties feel their needs are met.

Keep in mind there are possible gradients to achieving a positive outcome. In the context of this program, it is referred to as the Win/Win TO No Deal. Possible solutions have a range from Win/Win to No deal. This includes the possibility that both parties get most, or some of what they want. In some situations meaningful communication may not be possible, such as in traffic.

10. Anger Avoidance Short-term Strategy (STS):

This is called the Win/Win to No Deal STS. Encourage those participants dealing with anger avoidance to begin learning to use their anger in healthy ways. This strategy will later be used for other anger styles as well.

1. Anger is a normal emotion that everyone experiences.
2. Allow yourself to be angry when it is appropriate.
3. You are (and will be) a good person, even if you are angry.
4. Use your anger constructively. Open a dialogue with the other person, seeking Win/Win to No Deal Solutions as described above.
5. You always have the option to "feel the anger but choose the behavior".

11. Anger Avoidance Long-term Strategies (LTS):

A) Visualization LTS:

The following is a guided visualization that those who use the anger avoidance style may read to themselves daily. In the class we prefer to read it in conjunction with calming acoustical music. If anger avoidance is sufficiently represented in your anger management group, ask the participants to sit up comfortably, breathe easily, close their eyes, and read them the following:

"Visualize yourself interacting with someone who angers you. Notice how you begin looking when angry, how you feel, recognize your surroundings. Visualize yourself calmly and assertively using your anger well. You know this situation is important. Use your strength to face this situation with integrity and courage. You are assertive and fair. You politely and clearly explain the end result you want. You work through the situation, listening and responding appropriately. You seek a Win/Win to No Deal solution. Together, all parties find the best solution to this problem, implementing it to the benefit of all. You are a better person from this experience. You have learned from it, and move toward making a better future for yourself and the world. You feel refreshed and renewed at what you have accomplished."

Pass out a copy of this visualization, found in Appendix G, to any members desiring a copy.

B) Anger Avoider LTS:

Anger avoiders struggle with exhibiting their anger constructively as well as interacting with others who are angry. As a long-term strategy:

1. The avoider needs to learn to constructively verbalize their anger.
2. Using the ACT plan, they need to record their antecedent behaviors and the triggers associated with the behavior.
3. They need to verbalize and communicate the issues causing the anger. Such verbalization may involve the other party or solely themselves. When involving the other party, the avoider must practice inviting them to communicate their issues in a positive way, with the expectation the avoider will also have the opportunity to be heard.

The determination and assertiveness of the avoider is essential to the LTS. This is a cognitive behavioral strategy, which can be effective with other anger styles. As the program progresses, these strategies will be referred to again.

Session II: Anger Avoidance

    C) Assertiveness Training LTS:

Consider taking a course on constructive assertiveness training. Such a course should include elements of active listening and conflict resolution.

12. Anger Avoidance Positive Affirmation:

I acknowledge anger as one of my emotions,
Only using it in positive ways.
Knowing that every challenge is an opportunity,
I use my anger to help find Win/Win to No Deal Solutions.

13. Moral Values:

Sometimes people believe it is a burden living by a set of morals. They believe that by not doing what they want, they are missing out on life's opportunities. For instance, most people believe in the idea of fidelity within their marriage. An elicit relationship can have some appeal, yet the consequences of infidelity may be much higher than they at first appear to be. Aside from the risks of disease, pregnancy, and divorce, the consequences of acting against one's moral code are stress and negative thoughts. Psychologists call this cognitive dissonance. When acting against their moral code, they may repeat the behavior again and again, finding it easier to continue it.

Honesty: If you deal with people honestly and truthfully, they often treat you likewise. You should also consider dealing with yourself honestly. "Buy truth and do not sell it, get wisdom and instruction" (Proverbs 23:23).

Truthfulness: "You will know the truth and the truth will make you free" (John 8:32). In confrontations the truth frees us up emotionally to deal with the problem at hand. Rather than run from problems, we can work with all those involved to find solutions. Without truth, we are bound to our lies and deceptions. We are not free to act, as we must perpetuate our lies. By pursuing truth in all things, we follow a moral code that helps bring happiness.

Courage: When the Lord spoke to Joshua he said, "...Be strong and courageous! Do not tremble or be dismayed, for the Lord your God is with you wherever you go" (Joshua 1:9). "Be strong and let your heart take courage, all you who hope in the Lord" (Psalm 31:24).

These three moral values can combine when dealing with others. When one fails to embrace these moral values, the resultant relationships are built on uncertain ground. If you are an anger avoider, next time you feel the desire to leave an anger situation, begin by staying in the environment. In the case of a confrontation or argument, offer to listen, providing the other party agrees to listen to you as well. When your turn comes, honestly and constructively express your issues with the other party. Staying in a conflict helps you develop courage. Offering to listen elicits constructive conversation. Candid responses develop honest and truthful desire to resolve anger issues.

14. Homework:

- Continue using the Anger Control Today (ACT), as outlined in session I, emailing the observations to the counselor.
- Complete the optimism out-of-class Exercise 2.
- Continue using an Anger Affirmation daily as part of your overall anger management plan.

15. Music Therapy:

At the end of this and every remaining session, there is a seven minute seated stretching routine (yoga) followed by a three minute breathing exercise. During this portion of the program calming music should be played in the background. There is much scientific research discussing the emotional, mental, and physical benefits of music. For those interested in this research and why we recommend music as an adjunctive therapy for anger management, you may refer to Appendix M for more information.

16. Yoga:

Recommended in session I, exercise is an adjunctive long-term strategy. We recommend Yoga because it is easy to perform, has many health benefits, and can be practiced almost anywhere. The first time this six-move seated yoga exercise is performed, it may take a few minutes longer. Repeated each session, it becomes easier to remember and perform. Future sessions are for seven minutes. It is essential that group leaders perform the seated routine a sufficient number of times to be able to comfortably teach it to the members. Members may be given a copy of both the Yoga and the Diaphragmatic Breathing. Both are located in appendix Y.

Session II: Anger Avoidance

Perform this sitting routine doing the following:

- Ensure clothing is unrestrictive and comfortable. If necessary, it is appropriate to remove restrictive clothing such as jackets or loosen items such as belts.
- If possible, breathe through the nose the entire time.
- Use Diaphragmatic Breathing during the exercises. If members are unfamiliar with it, this breathing is explained in part 17 below. In future sessions it will always proceed the seated yoga exercises.
- Keep the tongue placed at the roof of the mouth, between the hard and soft palate.
- Only perform maneuvers that feel both comfortable and safe.
- Stop performing any maneuver if you experience dizziness, spotty vision, or shortness of breath.

The following is a seated stretching routine. This sequence of six moves can be completed in five to seven minutes. It can be performed by anyone able to move their arms and neck while seated. Each move flows into the next. The order of the moves is such that it promotes relaxation, with the brisker moves performed toward the end of the sequence. The last move (the Palm Flex) is designed to be performed slowly, with the breathing slow and focused. Performed in this manner, the sequence will relax the body and calm the mind.

1) Sitting Deep Breathing:

    This move is performed in two parts. Begin by interlocking the fingers under the chin with the palms facing down, and the elbows facing out at shoulder height. Keep the chin parallel to the floor while inhaling and raising the elbows as high as possible. Once the inhale is completed and the elbows are raised as high as possible, exhale while lowering the elbows back down to where they touch in front of the chest. Simultaneously push up the chin with the back of the interlocked fingers. The hands will form a single fist with the gaze directed upward. The pressure on the chin should be mild as you create a gentle stretch on the back of the neck.

2) Circular Neck Rotations:

    Sit upright. The tongue continues to touch the roof of the mouth. Rotate the neck in an oval pattern. One revolution should include both an inhale and an exhale. Because of the mechanics of the neck, it is safe to bring the head far forward, almost touching the chin to the upper chest. Due to the risk of neck injury, do not extend the head back as far as it will go during the rotation. This will cause the loop that the head travels to be oval shaped and more forward than back. After completing about seven revolutions in one direction, complete seven in the other. Both sides combined should take no more than a minute to complete.

3) Seated Upward Salute:

Place your hands above your head and interlock the fingers. While keeping the fingers interlocked, rotate the palms upward, facing the ceiling. Extend the arms as high as possible. Feel as if the spine is lengthening. If it feels comfortable, you may look up at the ceiling while performing the stretch. Otherwise continue keeping the gaze forward and the neck relaxed. Be careful to maintain your balance in the chair, avoiding leaning backward. Maintain this posture for four complete breathes or about twenty seconds.

4) Bent Arm Crosses:

Ensure first there is sufficient space between people in order to safely complete this exercise. Sit up straight and keep the gaze forward. Pay special attention to maintaining the neck and head relaxed during the exercise. Form both hands into light and relaxed fists, palms facing down, with both elbows kept at the height of the shoulders. While keeping the arms bent, push the elbows back as far as they will comfortably go. This motion is done with a small amount of speed, creating a light and gentle bounce. Kicking the elbows back in this fashion will lightly stretch the chest and shoulders. On each repetition, alternate crossing one wrist over the other, with both wrists and palms continuing to face the floor. Diaphragmatic breathing is not used in this exercise. Rather, the emphasis is on coordinating a short, light exhale with the backward kicking of the elbows. The breathing is more vigorous than with diaphragmatic breathing. Perform a total of fourteen to twenty repetitions. This should take less than thirty seconds to complete.

5) Seated Twisting with Heart Hands:

Place your feet solidly on the floor with your spine erect. Put your palms together with both of your thumbs touching the chest. Keep a small space between the palms as if you were holding something precious between them. Raise your elbows to a comfortable height, close to the height of your wrists and inhale. While maintaining this position, rotate your torso as far as you can to the left while exhaling. Inhale back to the center. Then exhale while rotating as far as you safely can to the right, keeping the spine erect and the hands over the chest. This is one repetition. Continue breathing diaphragmatically, completing up to ten full repetitions.

6) Palm Flex:

Place the hands comfortably on the knees with the palms facing upward, toward the ceiling. Using diaphragmatic breathing, fully open your hands stretching both palms as you inhale. Lightly close the hand, making a soft fist as you exhale. Be sure to feel the hand only lightly flexed on the exhale. This move helps counteract some of the physical tension in the hands. Do ten repetitions being sure to coordinate the movement with the diaphragmatic breathing.

17. Diaphragmatic Breathing (Abdominal Breathing):

A generalized strategy for calming and dealing with all types of anger is slow deep breathing, known as diaphragmatic breathing. At the end of each of these sessions diaphragmatic breathing will be performed. We recommend it be performed for about 3 minutes. When breathing, the inhales and exhales are for an equal amount of time. If you are alone and meditating, you might be able to hear your own heartbeat. If you develop the skill of hearing it as you breathe, you would inhale and exhale for an equal number of heartbeats. The breathing is performed with the eyes closed. It may also be used during the seated yoga exercises or as a short-term calming technique. In situations where it is used for calming, it may not be appropriate to close your eyes. It is generally performed with the hands folded gently on the lap (some schools of meditation will advise on particular hand gestures). Experienced practitioners could modify this technique according to their own understanding or their teacher's advice.

Read to members, or explain in your own words, the following:

"Begin by sitting up straight, comfortable, relaxed, and close your eyes. Lightly place the tip of the tongue at the top of the mouth, between the hard and soft palette. If possible, breathe only through the nose during the exercise. Always complete the breathing cycle by finishing on an exhale. Expel the air from the lungs, beginning the exercise on the inhale.

Normally it will be performed with the hands folded gently on the lap. In order to get a feel for breathing diaphragmatically, place one hand lightly on your upper chest and the other onto your belly. Now softly take a breath through your nose, allowing the air to fill up the lungs from bottom to top. The hand on your belly will move in and out with your breathing. The hand on your chest should not move until the top of the lungs begin to fill. Continue to breathe slowly, steadily, and evenly, with the inhale and exhale equal. The breath should feel calm, smooth, and relaxed."

For those who are interested, Appendix Y contains the following additional information regarding yoga and breathing:

- Scientific references regarding their benefits
- Additional suggested reading for more in-depth studies

Chapter 5

Session III: Sneaky Anger (Passive Aggression)

"A truth that's told with bad intent beats all the lies man can invent." - William Blake

1. Update and Review:

   A) Review with members any questions they may have regarding the previous session on anger avoidance. Members should have their Anger Control Today (ACT) files available, updating it when appropriate.
   B) Optimism week 2 review:

Review in-class scenario 2. What were some of the negatives and positives of the situation? Was the out-of-class exercise 2 more difficult or was it about the same as the scenario? Were they angry or frustrated with either list in its development. Remind participants a full optimism debriefing will occur in session IV.

2. Anger Control Today (ACT):

Conduct an Anger Control Review. This involves discussing with members the anger episode where they recorded their highest number on the anger meter. Do people feel there has been some progress in their individual anger management? The purpose of the review is the following:

- Familiarize members with using the ACT as an ongoing treatment plan.
- Help members identify the elements of the ACT, such as cues, triggers, and appropriate strategies.
- It is an opportunity for members to discuss their issues and listen to the issues of others.

When conducting this review, reinforce the positive solutions and strategies implemented by the members.

3. Session Overview:

- Positive Psychology: Optimism week 3
- Discuss Sneaky Anger (Passive Aggression)

4. Positive Psychology:

A) Optimism: week 3/scenario 3:

Give the members the third scenario, located in Appendix B. Looking at the situation and determining your frustration level is key to the management of anger. Read through the in-class scenario slowly. Then work through the questions. Refer back to the scenario whenever necessary. There are no right or wrong answers.

B) Optimism: week 3/Out of Class Exercise 3:

Give members the out-of-class exercise 3, located in Appendix B. Answer any questions members may have regarding completing the task. Members should not create an issue, simply record it if they are involved with or observe one. Then complete the fields of the questionnaire. If you are not directly involved, but observe a situation, you may have to rely on the physical cues of the people involved.

C) Gratitude is one of the strengths outlined in positive psychology, and is within our conscious control to improve. Improving your gratitude is likely to improve your overall happiness.[23] As stated before, happy people are less angry and less likely to respond to anger invitations and triggers. In regard to various anger styles, such as passive aggressive, the individual generally struggles with opportunities for being grateful to someone. These individuals tend to expend energy on undermining, which ultimately results in reducing their own happiness and appreciation for others.

The following gratitude exercise involves incorporating small gestures of gratitude throughout the week. Express them toward anyone to whom it is appropriate. Consider sending a text saying, "Thank you". Perhaps you might send a message to your spouse explaining you were thinking of them. You might send a card or an email to a family member or coworker. The important thing is to express gratitude. Do not comingle the exercise by expressing affection or romantic interest.

5. Sneaky Anger (Passive Aggression):

Passive aggression, also known as sneaky anger, is one of the masked (inward) anger styles. It has more overt action than the anger avoidance discussed in the last session. It is an indirect way of expressing anger, frustration, annoyance, or an unwillingness to perform some task. When people use this style, they tend to make others angry with them. It is a form of transference where one can say, "I am not the one who is angry, you are". In truth, the passive aggressor (PA) is the one who is angry first. The PA is usually not seen as the failure or cause of the problem, rarely exposing themselves to direct blame. Often times they appear as the most reasonable person in the room. This style of anger follows a general pattern, expressed in numerous ways:

1. The PA becomes annoyed or angry with someone else.
2. The PA uses some sort of subterfuge to cause the other person to become angry, annoyed, or frustrated.
3. The PA successfully transfers their anger to another person, placing the blame for the situation on the other person.

6. Patterns of Sneaky Anger:

The following are specific examples of how this anger is expressed:

A) Anger Transference: This form of sneaky anger does not require a task or request in order to elicit this response. When a PA participates in an anger invitation, they will attempt to transfer their anger onto the other person. This is usually played out in the following manner:

1. The PA will attempt to take the "high ground" by using a calming voice.
2. The PA will attempt to take the position of the reasonable person in the argument, pretending to listen while actually ignoring the other party.
3. The PA's physical gestures may be subdued, almost appearing above or beyond argument.
4. The result is that the other party becomes frustrated and eventually ends the argument. This gives the PA a sense of victory over the other.

B) Memory Lapse: It is the most common form of sneaky anger we have seen. It is used in the following manner:

1. A person makes a request of the PA.
2. The PA agrees to the request rather than create conflict.
3. The PA "forgets" to do the requested task.
4. The person making the request becomes angry or frustrated at the PA.
5. The person stops making requests of the PA, which is usually the desired result.

C) Feign Helplessness/Confusion: The PA will find reasons why the requested task is beyond them. They usually act as if the person making the request should already know this. It is performed as follows:

1. The PA will act as though the request requires more action/support by the person making the request.
2. The PA will continually request clarification of the instructions. This is intended to delay and frustrate the requestor.
3. The PA will eventually point out the best outcome is for the requestor to either do it themselves, or have the PA work with another who has more experience.
4. Eventually the requestor will do one or more of the following:
   - Withdraw the request.
   - Assign it to another person.
   - Do it themselves.

E) Refusal: With refusal one tends to say no, just to say no. It is a pattern of passive aggression more commonly exhibited by adolescents than adults. It really only qualifies as sneaky anger because the PA does not appear to be angry. It also follows the passive aggressive pattern of transference, causing the other party to become angry. An adult

Session III: Sneaky Anger (Passive Aggression)

PA will usually have developed a more sophisticated pattern that avoids any blame directed at them. This pattern works as follows:

1. Someone makes a request of the PA.
2. The PA refuses all requests.
3. If the PA actually wants to honor the request, they still refuse, but allow the other person to "convince" them. This way they do what they want after playing a mental tug of war.
4. If the PA does not want to do something, they just continue refusing. The goal is making the other person angry while maintaining power over themselves. This pattern is more about rebellion than managing incoming requests.

E) Perpetual Excuses; Delaying Tactics, Deflection:

The PA will combine a range of tactics to demonstrate their reasonableness, as well as the inability of the requestor to utilize the knowledge/skills properly.

1. Someone requests something of the PA.
2. The PA may make reasonable statements as to why they should not be assigned the task.
3. The PA may delay by continually asking for clarification, slow other previously assigned tasks' completion, or appear to be trying to create a better way to complete the task.
4. The PA will deflect the task by endless discussions on problems impeding completion. As the requestor offers solutions, the PA will argue (reasonably) why the solution will not work.
5. Ultimately the requestor will either deemphasize the task, move the completion date back, withdraw the request, or assign the task to someone else.

F) Withdrawal: In this pattern the PA will pretend not to hear the request. The PA may focus their attention onto something else, such as a TV show or an electronic device. This can occur as follows:

1. The PA is involved in some activity.
2. Someone requests something of the PA.
3. The PA pretends to not notice.

4. If the requestor persists, they may eventually coerce the PA into agreeing.

5. The PA then withdraws or sulks, poorly performing the task, or making the experience unenjoyable for all involved. The PA is giving the message that they may be coerced into doing something, but they do not have to do it with enthusiasm.

F) Self-Fulfilling Prophecy: In this pattern the PA outwardly agrees to the task while pointing out that the desired outcome will fail. The PA then sets about to undermine the given request in such a way as to guarantee the request's failure, without placing any of the blame upon the PA. When the task fails, the PA will be able to say that it was not their fault, they were following instructions and they warned the requestor of the inevitable failure. This can play out as follows:

1. Someone makes a request of the PA.

2. The PA informs the requestor that what they are asking either cannot be done or will fail.

3. The requestor then typically will give more detailed instructions on how to perform the given request.

4. The PA will find some way to subvert the request, such as by executing the letter rather than the spirit of the instructions.

5. Once the task meets with failure the PA will say that it was not their fault, they were given faulty instructions or insufficient tools.

6. Both the blame and the anger are displaced upon the requestor.

7. Benefits of Sneaky Anger:

When a PA is interacting with someone who has power or authority over them, sneaky anger can be beneficial. It is assumed that the PA is unable to directly attack the figure of authority. The PA may gain the benefit of resisting without a risk of direct confrontation. Sometimes the risks of direct confrontation are too great to justify making a stand. For instance, if a person were working for a particularly volatile and aggressive boss, they may use sneaky anger in order to resist the boss and make the boss look incompetent, hoping to get the boss fired. Sneaky anger can be used where the control is all one sided. Other potential benefits include avoiding responsibility, deflecting blame, being able to say no indirectly, and striking back at others emotionally without any apparent risk. The problems with sneaky anger lie in its use as a persistent style of anger.

Session III: Sneaky Anger (Passive Aggression)

8. Negative Consequences of Sneaky Anger:

- Isolation: The continued use of passive aggression can cause others to avoid the PA. Over time this can lead to limited social interaction, and we know such interaction is directly linked to both longevity and happiness.
- Negativity: All of that denying and negativity can lead to a negative outlook on life. Negative thoughts and words can contribute to a person's unhappy experience in life.
- Undervalue & Underachievement: The constant avoidance of requests and responsibilities can lead to the PA falling short of their potential, rarely completing projects of any note. Others begin to perceive them as incompetent, not giving them opportunities or responsibilities. In business, the PA forever relegates themselves, at best, to mid-management positions. In the private sector it can lead to unfavorable evaluations, corporate ostracizing, and getting fired. This in turn increases the PA's anger and stress, which can negatively affect their self-esteem. Low self-esteem is correlated to a host of other negative effects.
- Perpetuated Anger: By redirecting and transferring anger, PA's help to perpetuate a cycle of anger. Eventually the transferred anger gets aimed back at them via accusations and confrontations. The PA then redirects and transfers again, perpetuating a negative cycle of anger.
- Each time the PA uses sneaky anger, they subtly invalidate themselves both socially and emotionally. Over the long run, this can diminish one's self-confidence and deteriorate one's self-image.

9. Passive Aggressive Short-Term Strategy (STS):

The short-term goals of control, transference of anger, and manipulation are ultimately self-destructive. The PA's STS is an introspective analysis and modification of exhibited behavior. The following strategy plan is intended to be written down, recorded, and vigorously followed:

1. Identify the individual that caused the anger trigger.

2. Record the anger feelings elicited by the other person, i.e. resentment, jealousy, annoyance.

3. Aggressively pursue the request as if you had made the demand yourself. Treat it as your own idea.

4. Record the outcome of the request.

10. Passive Aggressive Long-Term Strategy (LTS):

This includes all of the STS and the following:

1. The PA working on their sneaky anger should record how they react to a request made by an individual that does not elicit a passive aggressive response.
2. Determine the difference between those whose requests set off a passive aggressive response and those who do not. See if there are obvious differences between the two types of individuals.
3. Exert effort to complete tasks that might elicit a passive aggressive response. Agree to complete those tasks, not because of who requested it, but because it will reflect on your skill and knowledge sets.
4. Participate in constructive communication with the intent of listening to the goals and opinions of the other party. Focus on the solution or in assisting the other individual in achieving their goal.
5. Develop skills in finding healthy compromise. Eliminate all or none thinking, such as "My way or the highway". This is much like the discussion in session II on Win/Win with an emphasis on effective listening.
6. Take responsibility for your anger. Acknowledge when someone makes you angry. This should result in you asking yourself "Why?"

11. Sneaky Anger Positive Affirmation:

I am an honest and loving person,
with the strength to face my fears.
I have valuable skills and talents,
with the courage to try my best.

12. Moral Values:

Sneaky anger can be a difficult pattern to change. Embracing the following morals can help ease one out of the pattern of this anger style:

Courage: Sometimes we know the right thing to do, yet it is difficult to do it. Cultivating courage can make the difference of doing the right thing or not when faced with a difficult situation. This is one of the reasons that so many different cultures and religions talk about the value of courage. "Wait for the Lord; be strong and let your heart take courage. Yes, wait for the Lord" (Psalms 27:14).

Integrity: Where courage is about the strength to do what is right, integrity is about actually doing it. Generally, people know what the right thing to do is in a given situation. Integrity comes from following the direction of that subconscious voice within us that knows right from wrong. "Let integrity and uprightness preserve me, for I wait for you" (Psalms 25:21).

Planning: It is one of the habits of the wise. Planning helps people determine their goals and plot out a course to achieve them. Good planning can help one develop more self-esteem, as they begin accomplishing their goals. The Bible advises a person to simultaneously plan while listening to that higher voice. "The mind of man plans his way, but the Lord directs his steps" (Proverbs 16:9).

Speaking Truth: To effectively use sneaky anger, one sometimes has to stretch the truth, or at least misdirect. The opening quote of this chapter by William Blake touches on this point. Sometimes PA's are masters of telling half-truths in order to manipulate a situation in their favor. It takes much courage and discipline to elevate one's intentions from that murky ground into speaking the truth. This also means being considerate of other's feelings. The truth should not be a weapon, but an instrument for better communication. "These are the things which you should do: speak the truth to one another; judge with truth and judgment for peace in your gates" (Zechariah 8:16).

13. Homework:

- Continue using the Anger Control Today (ACT) as outlined in session I, emailing the observations to the counselor.
- Complete the Optimism Out-of-Class Exercise 2.
- Begin the Gratitude Exercise.
- Continue using an Anger Affirmation daily as part of your overall anger management plan.

14. Yoga:

Run through the seated yoga stretches, following the instruction in part 16 of session II. In both this and the breathing exercise, include music that fits the anger management program criteria.

15. Diaphragmatic Breathing:

Perform the breathing exercise as outlined in part 17 of session II.

Chapter 6

Session IV: Anger Turned Inward

"Forgiveness does not change the past, but it does enlarge the future." -Unknown

1. Update and Review:

   A) Review with members any questions they may have regarding the previous session on sneaky anger. Members should have their Anger Control Today (ACT) file available, updating it when appropriate.
   B) Optimism Debriefing:

The reason for the first week assignment and exercise being focused on generally positive situations looking for positives, was training you to seek positives first. The last session assignment and exercise were to assist you to:

   • Seek the positives in a generally negative situation.
   • Train your thinking to develop counter arguments (positive) to your negative lists.
   • Give a more balanced perspective on negative situations, such as anger events.
   • Calmly assess and weigh the elements of an event.

Session IV: Anger Turned Inward

The expected outcomes were as follows:

- Those scoring more toward the pessimistic side would move closer to neutral (undecided) to somewhat positive.
- Optimistic people would move further toward optimistic scoring.
- Optimistic people would rerate the exercise and assignment as neutral or slightly positive. Pessimists would rate closer to neutral.

For long-term optimism skill development, continue performing exercise 3. In particular, focus on listing the core negatives of a situation and the counter arguments. A word of caution: people can fall into the habit of quickly listing the negatives, adding a quick counter argument, and then skipping over the importance of the counter argument. This essentially nullifies its effectiveness. Instead, while working on this skill, it is best to list all the primary negatives first, then list all the counter arguments.

2. Anger Control Today (ACT):

Conduct an Anger Control review, discussing with the members the anger episode where they recorded their highest number on the anger meter. The purpose of the review is the following:

- Familiarize members with using the ACT as an ongoing treatment plan.
- Help members identify the elements of the ACT, such as cues, triggers, and appropriate strategies.
- It is an opportunity for members to discuss their issues and listen to the issues of others.

When conducting the review, reinforce the positive solutions and strategies implemented by the members.

3. Session Overview:

The following are the main points of this session:

- Positive Psychology: Self-Forgiveness VSS training
- Anger Turned Inward Anger Style
- Inward Anger Short and Long-Term Strategies

4. Positive Psychology:

Introduced in chapter 1, self-control is one of the 24 listed Virtue/Strength/Skills (VSS). It can be augmented by the acquisition of specific skill sets. All short and long-term strategies involve some level of self-control. When a person removes themselves from a situation (LEAP/session V) that involves self-control skills. By developing positive skills, such as self-control, one also acquires gratification.

   A) Self-Forgiveness: Week 1/Scenario 1:

Pass out self-forgiveness scenario 1, located in Appendix C. Members should read it and answer the proceeding questions.

   B) Self-Forgiveness: Week 1/Out-of-Class Exercise 1:

Give members the out of class exercise 1. Answer any questions they may have regarding completing the task. Screen any questions that are best answered at the debriefing in session VI.

5. Anger Turned Inward:

Caveat: All of the Anger Turned Inward (ATI) patterns could potentially be related to other problems and disorders such as depression, negative self-image, ODD, or PTSD. One may have to treat the person in the context of these other disorders. In such cases the anger may only be a symptom of or a trigger related to those disorders.

This is the last of the masked anger styles being presented in this course. In this style, a person generally feels the anger but it is either directed at themselves, or transmuted into another negative emotion and then directed at themselves. Sometimes people who exhibit this pattern do not admit they are angry, yet they will treat themselves poorly. Manifestations of this anger style can accompany feelings of disgust, inadequacy, and failure. This anger style can be manifested with almost all other anger styles, especially less overt ones such as shame based or sneaky anger. It is least likely to be coupled with anger styles that overtly direct the anger outward, such as excitatory anger.

Session IV: Anger Turned Inward

6. Five Primary Patterns of Anger Turned Inward:

A) Self-Blame: People with this pattern tend to believe that if something goes wrong, then it must be their fault. They may call themselves names, believe they are incapable, and expect to be blamed for whatever goes wrong. Their sense of blame goes beyond responsibility for their own thoughts and actions. If a friend gets into a fight, they should have calmed them down. They believe that it is their own incompetence or lack of action that is the root cause of most problems.

B) Self-Sabotage: Self saboteurs may have goals and enthusiasm, but they can never get the important things accomplished. Many believe they do things wrong and need to be told how to do it right. This creates a complex pattern of shame, anger, rebellion, resentment, and paralysis. They may feel guilt at a simple request to change something, taking it as a command. They may try, feel inadequate to the task, and then fail. This failure is not from lack of ability, but from a sense of internal rebellion. This rebellion can become an internal dialogue which causes them to resist their own goals and ideas. They may also exhibit confusion as their mind races to complete a goal they really do not want to complete. For some, this takes on the form of paralysis. This is caused by cognitive dissonance from the dichotomous mental scripts that say, one must accomplish some task while at the same time one must NOT do it in order to express one's feelings of rebelliousness.

C) Self-Neglect: This is a pattern into which caregivers often times fall. It starts by them having more things they must do for others and less time for themselves. Eventually this can become a way of life. When it starts to become the overriding way they suppress their anger, it becomes a problem. Since they are doing what everyone wants, there are very few conflicts, and they do not have time to be angry. Eventually they must come to realize that their self-sacrifice is turning into self-abuse. This pattern of self-neglect can foster the idea that a person is not as worthy or important as others. Often times, the self-neglector's basic needs are not being adequately met as well.

This pattern can morph into other anger styles. For instance, a caregiver may develop passive aggression toward other potential caregivers who are not pulling their weight. This might be where only one sibling is caring for an elderly parent. They may feel the situation is the fault of the care-receiver and come to blame and resent them. These negative feelings can cause the caregiver to become abusive or aggressive toward the care-receiver.

D) Self-Attack: This fourth pattern relates to the idea that one must be punished or that one deserves to be treated badly. Such behavior can manifest in the following ways:

- Hitting walls
- Kicking things
- Banging one's head
- Cutting oneself
- Scratching symbols into one's skin or creating wounds
- "Accidently" harming oneself when one is angry
- Constantly placing oneself into dangerous situations

Sometimes such people seek out abusive relationships or difficult partners. Sometimes there is the concept of an internal "punisher" as part of their psyche. Many of these people have internalized a series of harmful or dangerous situations from their past. What causes some people to internalize and displace such behavior while not affecting others is unknown. Such self-destructive behavior generally touches on a number of disorders beyond this anger style.

E) Self-Destruction: Extreme shame and extreme anger can lead to polarized world views, with all or nothing thinking. Such people may perceive themselves as all bad, taking no praise or love from others. If a participant has expressed a desire to kill themselves, refer them to depression/crisis counseling.

7. Benefits of Anger Turned Inward:

If a person makes a bad decision or harms someone in some way, it might be healthy to be angry with oneself. That negative feeling may be there to reinforce something one just learned, helping one to make better future decisions. A conscionable person might have a constructive amount of guilt, shame, or anger over having done something wrong. It is important to notice the anger and/or the accompanying negative emotion. Use them as an indicator that the problem might lie inward with oneself, and then adjust one's behavior accordingly.

8. Negative Consequences of Anger Turned Inward:

When anger turns inward it can manifest in a variety of destructive ways. It ranges from patterns of self-criticism, to self-neglect, self-mutilation, and even suicide. All of these patterns can include a certain amount of unhappiness, stress, and cognitive dissonance.

Session IV: Anger Turned Inward

9. Anger Turned Inward Short-Term Strategies (STS):

Self-blame: One of the underlying problems with self-blame is the negative feelings of self-worth that can arise. This is the result of an unhealthy perception of themselves and/or situations. They tend to only notice the negative related to themselves, totally unaware of the positive. They blow negative events out of proportion, further reinforcing their negative self-image. They must develop thinking patterns that allow them to become aware of the positive in any given situation, as well as all the positive behaviors that occurred before any singular negative event. They also need to develop a healthier perspective on events, allowing them to see it in context. The reduction in negative thinking, the increased awareness of associated positive events, and the ability to place things in perspective, usually result in a healthier self-image. This leads to improved feelings of self-worth. In time this produces a reduction of self-blame to a point where there is less or no need to blame others.

A) Inward Anger STS:

1. For any level of explosive, even self-harming anger, move away from the trigger. The trigger may also be a place or situational. Use LEAP from session V.
2. Use Diaphragmatic Breathing to calm.
3. Calm Discussion. Invite others to talk, listening first with the agreement that you will then be listened to as well. This may also be an internal discussion with oneself.
4. Perception and Perspective. People get angry with one another or become angry. Take only your part of the responsibility. When you think negative thoughts, push for a counter argument.

B) Positive Replacement STS:

1. Carry something with you where you can record your thoughts, such as a cell phone, palm computer, or a note card.
2. Every time you have a negative thought regarding yourself, stop and replace it with a counter thought.
3. Notice any positive elements of the situation, such as if you were multi-tasking or solving an important problem at the time, and thus distracted. What were the

positive events that led up to this one? How many times did things go well or did you perform them correctly before this perceived mistake?

4. Put the situation into perspective. Were you or anyone hurt? Will the event dramatically alter anyone's life? If the event was not so significant, move on. If it was life altering, learn from the event. Take the positive with you and take steps to prevent the negative from happening again.

Example: If you were walking and bumped into a corner you might think, "I am such a klutz". Stop instead and say, "I am a coordinated and aware person". Be certain to notice any positive elements of the situation. Was it a big deal? If all you did was drop a pen, pick it up and move on with your day. If you are going to assign some degree of negativity to yourself, give greater weight to the positive elements you brought to the situation. This will help develop a more positive opinion of yourself.

10. Inward Anger Long-term Strategies (LTS):

A) Goal Completion LTS:

1. Each day set and record tasks you wish to complete, creating a tangible to-do list.
2. Work on one task at a time until it is completed. If the task takes more than 30 minutes to complete, divide it into 30 minute "chunks".
3. Whenever you complete a task on your list, physically check it off of your list.
4. After you have completed tasks, or a 30 minute portion, take a short break totaling about 10 minutes per hour. Use part of this time to recognize the task you properly completed. Re-live the experience of completing the task, and notice how it felt to complete it.
5. Find some small and healthy way to immediately reward yourself for completing each task or "chunk". Examples include a cup of coffee, a healthy drink, or meditating. Consider writing a short email to a friend or loved one. Let them know you are being productive and wish them a good day.
6. Continue to proceed in this fashion until all of your allotted work time has been used.

If a member has difficulty with this strategy, the Group Leader or counselor should ensure the member is making reasonable to-do lists and ensure that the goals are realistic. Also ensure that the member is implementing proper rewards and reliving the completion of tasks.

Session IV: Anger Turned Inward

    B) Inward Focus LTS:

        1. Each time you are helping another or facilitating another's needs to be met, ask yourself if your same need is also being met.
        2. If the answer is no, and it is possible to so do, share or join in the activity that you are facilitating. If it is impossible or unreasonable to share in the activity, consider meeting your needs directly after providing that same care to another.

Example: If you cook and provide a meal for another and you are also hungry, consider eating the meal with them. If you are bathing a sick loved one, after they are finished and placed safely in bed, consider taking a bath yourself.

    C) Self-Image LTS:

        1. They must be made aware they have been neglecting themselves.
        2. They must find the incorrect beliefs that drive this pattern.
        3. They should learn to deal with the guilt of saying "no" when they must do so. They must learn to see things in the context of a broader view, rather than a narrower, all or nothing lens.
        4. There must be breaks throughout the day for the caregiver to spend time on themselves and strictly for themselves. Such breaks might involve reading, taking a bubble bath, or eating a nice meal alone.
        5. Having purpose and meaning in life raises happiness. This is especially true if they can begin working on personal life dreams and goals.

11. Affirmation:

I ask for help when I need it.
I recognize that each day is an opportunity to experience deep joy.
I have great value and am filled with love.
I turn that love both toward myself and others.

12. Moral Values:

The following moral values can be applied toward lessening the effects of Anger Turned Inward. Since these are positive moral values, they also can impact many other aspects of a person's life, including lessening the effects of some other anger styles.

Non-judging: This fosters better interpersonal relationships and frees up energy on more worthy endeavors. Can you judge yourself in a healthy and balanced manner? Can you see the positive in things? Are you truly placing things into proper perspective? "Do not judge so that you will not be judged. For in the way you judge, you will be judged; and by your standard of measure, it will be measured to you." (Mathew 7:1-2)

Enjoying Life: Often times people who harm themselves and want to end it all, feel little to no joy in their lives. They often fail to see the beautiful things in life. Because of complex chemicals in the brain, people who are depressed literally see the world as less vibrant and colorful. Enjoying life is one of the first steps to living life. "There is nothing better for a man than to eat and drink and tell himself that his labor is good. This also I have seen that it is from the hand of God." (Ecclesiastes 2:24)

Using Positive Speech: The value and power of positive speech was discussed in chapter 2 and is also in appendix S. Changing the words we use can, over time, improve our whole quality of life. "An evil man is ensnared by the transgression of his lips, but the righteous will escape from trouble." (Proverbs 12:13) Taken literally, this passage implies that people make their life more difficult by what they say.

Self-worth: If a person believes in an all-powerful and benevolent creator that must include the knowledge that they were created by such a being. Improving our self-image improves our self-worth. Our self-worth is bolstered by knowing we were created in the image of God. "Then God said, Let Us make man in Our image, according to Our likeness…" (Genesis 1:26). Many Scriptures point to the unique value of humankind as a creator of both flesh and spirit. "Or do you not know that your body is the temple of the Holy Spirit who is in you, whom you have from God, and that you are not your own?" (1 Corinthians 6:19-20). Being claimed by God means you have both value and worth.

13. Homework:

- Continue using the Anger Control Today (ACT), as outlined in session I, emailing observations to the counselor. Counselors should continue reviewing and responding to these emails before the next session begins. Continue using the ACT in this fashion throughout all of the remaining sessions.
- Begin the week 1 Self-control VSS homework.

Session IV: Anger Turned Inward

- Continue the gratitude exercise.
- Continue to use an anger affirmation daily as part of the overall anger management plan.

14. Progressive Relaxation Exercise:

Incorporated into Appendix Y is a Progressive Relaxation Exercise. It is intended to be audio recorded and then played back while one is either sitting or lying down comfortably. For members not adept at meditation, it is a way to take 10 minutes in order to relax. Distribute (uplink, email) a copy of this exercise to any members who would like to try it.

15. Yoga:

Run through the seated yoga stretches, following the instructions in part 16 of session II. In both this and the breathing exercise, include music that fits the anger management program criteria.

16. Diaphragmatic Breathing:

Perform the breathing exercise as outlined in part 17 of session II.

Chapter 7

Session V: Sudden Anger

"Whoever is slow to anger has great understanding, but he who has a hasty temper exalts folly." (Proverbs 14:29)

1. Update and Review:

A) Review with members any questions they may have regarding the previous session on Anger Turned Inward. Members should have their Anger Control Today (ACT) file available, updating it when appropriate.

B) Self-Forgiveness week 1 review:

The situations involving others were to have some level of blame. This exercise should prepare members for looking at identifying and assigning blame. Have members share insights regarding their assignment.

C) Gratitude Exercise Review:

Over the course of the previous two weeks, participants should have found moments to express gratitude to family and friends either in person, by a quick text, email, or call. The purpose of the exercise was to provide an opportunity for members to identify and strengthen their important relationships. Inward anger styles, such as passive aggression, often lead to strained personal relationships and reduced social contacts. Developing genuine appreciation (gratitude) for others can counteract some of the negative consequences of angry behaviors and improve happiness. Focus on the following questions:

- What was the reaction of the person who received the gratitude?
- What were the general responses?
- How did the participant feel after they expressed gratitude?
- Did they feel happier? Was that day a bit better?

2. Anger Control Today (ACT):

Conduct an Anger Control Review following the instructions in part 11 of session I. Continue with the proceeding questions:

- Highest number on the scale?
- Anger Categories?
- Anger Cues?
- Triggering Event and Antecedent Behaviors?
- Strategies used to control the anger?

3. Session Overview:

The following are the main points of this session:

- Positive Psychology: Self-Forgiveness week 2, Self-Control week 1.
- Review personal anger cues.
- Learn about Sudden Anger and LEAPing into time-outs.

4. Positive Psychology:

A) Self-forgiveness week 2:

- Distribute the Self-Forgiveness week 2/Scenario 1. Have members read it and answer the proceeding questions.
- After completing scenario 1, distribute the week 2/Scenario 2. Have members read it and answer the accompanying questions.

B) Self-Forgiveness: Week 2/Out-of-Class Exercise 2:

Give members the out-of-class exercise 2. Answer any questions they may have regarding completing the task. Screen any questions that are best answered at the debriefing in the next session.

C) Self-Control: Week 1/Out-of-Class Exercise 1:

Self-control relies, in part, on the ability to put temporary restrictions on oneself. It is necessary in the implementation of both short and long-term strategies. Simply initiating a time-out (LEAP) is an exercise in self-control. Further development of this Virtue/Strength/Skill (VSS) is therefore a great benefit to members. Give members the out-of-class exercise 1, located in Appendix D. Answer any questions they may have regarding completing the task. Screen any questions that are best answered at the debriefing in session VIII.

5. Sudden Anger:

In this style of anger a person knows they are angry or have an anger issue. This is generally described as the one with the "short fuse". They express their anger by yelling, breaking things, threatening, or attacking others. Like a summer storm, they are quick to arrive and leave. The energy they expend in the exhibition of the anger tends to wear them down. Like all the explosive styles of anger, they are not just a danger to themselves, but to those around them. People who express this anger style almost universally tell us that their anger comes on all of a sudden, with no warning. To them it feels as if they lose control and it is imperative that they act out immediately. Triggers for these individuals are not necessarily more common than other anger styles. The following are the underlying issues for these individuals:

- How to manage anger constructively.
- Emotional ranges and perspective. Situations tend to be seen with greater importance or weight than called for.
- High fueled episodes help to focus everyone involved onto the anger and the needs of the person acting out.
- In the case where the trigger involves another person, by exploding the individual eliminates other possible actions.

There are antecedent events to the outburst. However, the duration between the initial triggering event and anger activation is generally short.

6. Benefits of Sudden Anger:

Sudden anger has value whenever one must meet an immediate threat, and there is no time to pause. In such a situation one must react or be harmed. In a classic "fight or flight" scenario, sudden anger is a valid tactic. Example: one might be protecting another from an attacker, dodging an incoming blow, or using that burst of accompanying adrenaline to jump out of harm's way. Both fear and anger activate the Sympathetic Nervous System (SNS), giving one an immediate boost in energy. Additionally, the individual's physical tension looks for a release which promotes a return to a calmer state.

7. Negative Consequences of Sudden Anger:

Sudden Anger can damage any relationship and disrupt social ties. Jobs, friends, partners, property, and liberty can all be lost. The confrontation that some get into as a result of this anger style can also lead to injury to oneself or others. As an exercise write down what session members call out as the many examples of the potential negative consequences of sudden anger.

8. Out of Control:

It is reasonable to question why some people do not just control their anger considering that the vast majority of people are able to do so. As was cited earlier, about half of personality traits, such as anger, are attributable to genetics. Exactly how this interacts with macro-effects, such as behavior, is not well known. We know that some brains are not as good at controlling anger and aggression. For example, some people have an overactive limbic system. This causes their brain to feel emotions both rapidly and intensely.[24] Some people have weaker activation of the prefrontal cortex, and thus less impulse control.

Having implemented our program in a prison environment, we have observed many masters of "urban" psychology. One phrase that some of our participants brought to us was, "Even a monkey knows which tree it can climb." Those people who express themselves with a sudden anger style, almost never explode at (climb on) people they believe will hurt them. Though they all tell us they have no control once they are angry, most of them do have discretion on or toward whom they will explode. For years we have lived in South Central Florida, the lightning capital of the world. The abruptness of the summer storms there are legendary, but there are always signs that one is coming.

People who express the sudden anger style have warning signs. These individuals are generally either not taking the time to recognize the cues and triggers of their anger, or don't really care. If the result of these explosions is usually to get what they want and a physical release, they will not necessarily be overly concerned with the identification of triggers. Often times they experience a frustration or a series of frustrations. Then they ignore the warning signs that they are becoming angry. They may come home late for dinner after being stuck in traffic. Then they walk through the hallway and bump into a child's toy. Suddenly they pick up the toy and throw it against the wall as hard as they can and start yelling. In effect, an entire day's frustration is being taken out at once. Therein lies the whole problem. In this instance, anger is not perceived as a signal but rather a solution to their frustration. After an outburst they feel better, except now they have to fix the wall and apologize for screaming again. Let us look at where this all goes wrong and what can be done to correct it.

9. Medication and Sudden Anger:

In the cases where someone's sudden anger is a real danger to themselves and others, medication may assist with minimizing the severity of the emotional shift that would precede the anger event. As with all symptom management strategies that involve a pharmacological component, behavioral management strategies must also be incorporated. Sudden anger is manageable, and many clients are able to learn to gain control over their anger using anger management techniques.

10. Explosive Anger Exercise and Discussion:

In session I, myth #4 it was discussed that venting anger only teaches one to get good at expressing the anger. Venting anger rehearses it. Feeding emotions with outward actions only fans the flames that fuel those emotions. In effect one trains themselves to be more explosive. One tries to feel better by letting off steam. Instead they misapply cognitive and behavioral therapies, rehearsing a negative event over and over.

Group Exercise: Research shows that as people get older, they tend to have less explosive outbursts. Why do older people not succumb to explosive anger as often as they did before? Have members share and discuss their answers to this question.

11. Sudden Anger Short-Term Strategies (STS):

   A) LEAP Time-out STS:

Anger invitations were discussed in part 10 of session I. It is important that members who are dealing with an explosive anger style be aware of when anger invitations are being extended toward them. Briefly review what an anger invitation is. In session I a time-out was presented as a short-term strategy. One's awareness of anger cues and anger invitations combine with the immediate use of a time-out. This is an especially important tool to help manage sudden anger. To make it easier to recall during a stressful event, we have the following mnemonic:

LEAP when your anger cues begin to give you a warning.

(L) Losing control: anger cues are mounting. You might lose control.
(E) Exit the situation: Remove yourself so that you have time to think more clearly.
(A) Adjust yourself: Find a way to relax. Take a walk. Use your effective short-term techniques.
(P) Problem solve: Identify the root of the problem. From a list of possible choices, seek a positive solution to achieve the best possible outcome.

Most episodes of explosive anger are, in part, due to the individual's improper perspective of the situation. (Was the toy on the floor that much of an issue?) In addition to perspective, the person needs to pause and consider the possible ramifications of an anger episode. Do they want to harm someone else or potentially themselves?

B) Sudden Anger STS involving others:

1. Step away (LEAP): Go for a walk, step outside. Be sure to tell the individual (if applicable) that you need to step away for a few moments.
2. Perspective: Put the event in perspective. Is the trigger worth it to expend the energy? Is there something else affecting this event; something that happened, or you are anticipating to happen?
3. Communication: Talk it through with yourself. If appropriate, speak out loud (not yelling, conversational voice). What are the circumstances to which you are reacting? What are the ramifications of exploding?
4. Do not reenter the environment until you feel the same level of energy you would normally feel. To say "calm down" is not enough. It is vital to know what your calm state feels like, so you know when you have achieved it. If you need to, use your anger meter. You left at a 4, going toward a 5, and now you rate yourself at a 2, maybe 3.

Once you have initiated a time-out, it is important to use one of the learned short-term techniques to decompress. Drugs, alcohol, or picking arguments do not solve the root problem, and usually make it worse. Once you have truly relaxed and it is prudent to do, go back and solve the problem. If another person is involved, find a Win/Win to No Deal solution. Be both proactive and positive with your destiny.

It is important to add this additional caveat; for some people, walking away from a confrontation is a trigger. In the case of some sneaky anger (passive aggressive) people, walking away may cause them to ruminate about what they should have done in the confrontation. The act of engaging a time-out might actually be counterproductive to their individualized cognitive therapeutic techniques, as they may use it as an avoidance behavior.

C) Sudden Anger STS Without Direct Contact:

In situations where there is no direct contact with another person, you must first consider perspective. As an example, if you are cut off on your drive to work, this can trigger an anger episode.

1. The first step in the STS is to calm down.
2. Breathe. Focus on speaking to yourself rather than yelling about the situation.
3. Remember where you are going and put the proper perspective on the situation. Do you want to risk your job for the situation?
4. Consider the counter argument to nearly being in an accident. You were not in an accident and no one was hurt.

12. Sudden Anger Long-Term Strategies (LTS):

A) Anger Cues LTS:

Group leaders should ensure that each member has written down their personal anger triggers, as well as antecedent events and behaviors. The ACT sheet is instrumental in this task. Be especially mindful that members with explosive anger styles are able to articulate all of their individual cues that they are becoming angry. Ensure that each member has their individual anger cues recorded in their ACT file. As a review exercise of part 9 of session I, have members give examples of anger cues in each of the four categories: physical, behavioral, emotional, and cognitive.

B) Communicating Calmly LTS:

Retraining oneself to communicate calmly is a long-term strategy. In some confrontations, calm communication helps to prevent escalation of the situation. This communication can include speaking to oneself. As in active listening, calm communication helps to foster an exchange of information between both parties. Such communication is designed to help one maintain their calm and encourages the other party to do likewise. Record the following behaviors:

- If inside, sit down. If outside, gently fold your hands in front of you.
- Speak in quiet tones, but loud enough to be understood.
- Do not swear or use profanity.
- If dealing with another person, work toward Win/Win to No Deal solutions.
- Do not exaggerate or lie.
- In order to gain perspective, listen to what others have to say. This may also just be speaking with yourself.
- Perform diaphragmatic breathing, with inhales slightly longer than exhales.

Practice these behaviors sufficiently until they become the reacting behavior set. Whenever it is prudent to remain in a confrontation, attempt to use these behaviors. If you have a confrontation with another individual, afterward record your thoughts regarding it. Analyze both what you did correctly and what could use improvement. Remember that learning to use new behaviors takes practice and diligence. Sometimes it feels as if one is moving two steps forward, then one step back. In addition to cue and trigger recognition, it is important to consider the antecedent events or behaviors. Identifying if the causal triggers were the trigger itself, or a culmination of events, is critical to developing control. For most, if the individual can extend the time between episodes, long-term management will be successful.

The primary issue for participants with sudden anger is they improve, and then they back-slide. This sense of control (improving) to loss of control (back-sliding) is a natural cycle to improvement of long-term control. As an example, if the member exhibits sudden anger at least once a day, their initial goal may be to have an episode every two days. This goal will continue until they have gone a week without an episode. If the member gets to one week and then has an episode, they should go back to where they were continuously successful (i.e. every four days), and work up from there. Again, this is referred to as back-chaining.

13. Affirmation:

I listen for and am aware of my personal anger cues.
My anger cues are signal to be to be aware of my anger.
I LEAP into time-outs to stay calm and in control.
I live healthy and embrace a joy-filled life.

14. Moral Values:

The following moral values can be applied toward lessening the effects of sudden anger. Since these are positive moral values, they also can impact many other aspects of a person's life, including lessening the effects of some other anger styles. For instance, patience is a virtue that can help with explosive styles of anger, as well as many of the others.

Patience: patience is the space between stimulus and response in a time-out. It is that virtue that buys one the time they need to make an optimal decision. While it is valid that some decisions require an instantaneous response, the overwhelming majority of significant decisions in a person's life allow some time for reflection. Patience affords one that time to choose from among many possibilities. "But the fruit of the Spirit is love, joy, peace, patience, kindness, goodness, faithfulness, gentleness, self-control; against such things there is no law" (Galatians 5:22-23).

Vigilance: this is a key component in implementing any cognitive behavioral strategy. Vigilance is what helps a person to remain focused. Bad habits can be hard to break. Vigilance helps a person to apply new strategies to bad habits, whenever they occur. Real problems have a tendency to appear at inopportune moments. Vigilance ensures we are on the alert to meet the challenge when it arrives. "Be of sober spirit, be vigilant. Your adversary, the devil, prowls around like a roaring lion, seeking someone to devour" (1 Peter 5:8).

Peace: peace is the space that allows us to enjoy the good life we have earned. Without peace, an enjoyable life can become entangled in needless and unpleasant conflicts. Though some conflict is beneficial, peace is the breath of fresh air that gives us additional freedom to enjoy the moment. "Depart from evil and do good, seek peace and pursue it" (Psalms 34:14). "Blessed are the peacemakers, for they shall be called sons of God" (Mathew 5:9).

15. Homework:

- Continue to use the Anger Control Today (ACT), recording events as outlined in session 1, emailing observations to the counselor.
- Continue using an Anger Affirmation as part of the overall anger management plan.
- For members dealing with any form of Explosive Anger, memorize the LEAP method of time-out and/or Communicating Calmly.
- Begin the week 1 Self-Control skill training homework.
- Begin the week 2 Self-Forgiveness skill training homework.

Session V: Sudden Anger

16. Yoga:

Run through the seated yoga stretches, following the instructions in part 16 of session II. In both this and the breathing exercise, include music that fits the anger management program criteria.

17. Diaphragmatic Breathing:

Perform the breathing exercise as outlined in part 17 of session II.

Chapter 8

Session VI: Shame-Based Anger

"Nothing gives one person so much advantage over another as to remain always cool and unruffled under all circumstances". -Thomas Jefferson in a letter to Isaac McPherson (1813)

1. Update and Review:

A) Review with members any questions they may have regarding the previous session on Sudden Anger. Members should have their Anger Control Today (ACT) file available, updating it when appropriate.

B) Self-forgiveness Debriefing:

In all of the scenarios and exercises, the primary focus was on the assignment of blame, which fosters guilt. The questions were designed to make you ask, "Is blame really needed?". The act of self-forgiving is based on how self-blame and guilt were assigned by you. Wherever in the exercises you assigned some self-blame (to yourself) you need to forgive yourself. People with poor situational perspective, and/or poor self-image, may fall into a negative pattern of blaming themselves. By improving your perception of the various arguments and your perspective on anger situations, you may not need to assign any blame.

Session VI: Shame-Based Anger

The week 1 exercises were designed to teach:

- There are gradients of blame that lead to guilt.
- Not all situations with a negative element require the assignment of blame.
- If some form of blame is assigned, it can be shared.

These skills were then expanded to include better perspective and other ways of considering events that are normally viewed as negative. In the week 2 scenarios, the first set of questions were designed to direct your focus toward minimizing blame and thus develop less potential guilt. The second set of questions were to help you get a different perspective. By changing the assignment of blame you develop the ability to redirect the negative elements in a situation or incident. As you start to develop a healthier self-image, self-forgiveness becomes possible.

By practicing the skill of healthy situational analysis, you eliminate or minimize guilt, shame, and blame. You should continue applying the questions in the out-of-class exercise 2 to any situations where you assign yourself blame.

C) Self-Control Week 1 Review:

In the first week we worked on a very basic level of self-control. We chose a daily task and a reward at completion of the task. This adds a level "one" of self-control. The debriefing of self-control occurs in session VIII.

2. Anger Control Today:

Conduct an Anger Control Review following the instructions in part 11 of session I. Continue with the proceeding questions:

- Highest number on the scale?
- Anger Categories?
- Anger Cues?
- Triggering Event and Antecedent Behaviors?
- Strategies used to control the anger?

3. Session Overview:

The following are the main points of this session:

- Positive Psychology: Self-Control week 2
- Learn about Shame-Based Anger (SBA).

4. Positive Psychology:

A) Self-Control Week 2/Out-of-Class Exercise:

Give members the out-of-class exercise 2. The previous exercise is now reversed. Members identify something they want, and delay getting it until the completion of a self-assigned task. Answer any questions members may have regarding the exercise. Screen any questions that are best answered at the debriefing in session VIII.

5. Shame-Based Anger (SBA):

Negative emotions such as guilt, worthlessness, and insecurity are the driving forces of this anger style. When these negative feelings toward the self are internalized, they can become a trigger for a defensive angry reaction. The cycle appears as follows:

1. A person has one or more negative emotions toward themselves as a trigger for shame.
2. A person or event triggers any one of these negative emotions, which in turn cause shame.
3. This triggered shame causes the person to feel or experience anger.
4. This anger then activates an aggressive defensive protocol. It can take the form of the person lashing out at the triggering person with abusive words and violent behaviors, or becoming angry toward a triggering event.
5. Afterwards the person may feel guilty for having lashed out or for having their "shame" or weakness exposed. This can increase their guilt and lower their threshold of sensitivity to further triggering events, creating a cycle.
6. The person experiencing the anger feels they must immediately react. Consequently, this entire sequence can come about quickly. Because each new round creates more guilt, this cycle can self-perpetuate.

Session VI: Shame-Based Anger

6. Benefits of Shame-Based Anger:

The opposite emotions to shame are confidence and pride. If shame can push a person toward positive, prideful acts, then it has value. Shame may also be an indicator that one has done something wrong and needs to change for the better. Example: a person may do some poor quality work for their company and their boss may then point it out to them. A person who normally takes pride in their work might use that as motivation to work harder or better. Their overall performance may then improve as they strive to rise above their previously substandard work. Any time one feels ashamed, if it is used to drive toward something positive, the shame has served a purpose.

7. Negative Consequences of Shame-Based Anger:

Like all of the explosive anger styles, the effects of this anger are visible. Relationships can be damaged and social ties disrupted. The risk of injury to self or others is also a possibility, along with consequences such as arrest, loss of job, and reduced income. Continued use of this anger style can compound a person's negative emotions, such as shame. This can lead to more feelings of negative self-worth and reduced self-esteem.

8. Justification/Self-Image Masking:

Shame is a powerful emotion. The individual usually calls for some kind of defense when they feel shame. Common ego defenses include the following:

1. Addiction: Sometimes a person might turn to drugs, alcohol, or some compulsive behavior in order to mask negative feelings.
2. Arrogance: Sometimes people tell themselves that they are above these feelings or sorts of people as a way to deal with the shame they feel.
3. Denial: Sometimes people pretend they are not really hurt in order to defend themselves against emotional pain. It also is an attempt to show strength in the presence of others.
4. Withdrawal: Here a person removes themselves from the person or situation that triggered their shame. For instance anger avoidance and shame-based anger could combine in this way.
5. Anger: This is also called narcissistic rage. A person may feel the reason they are ashamed is because of some attack directed toward them. Because they genuinely feel attacked, they feel justified in lashing out in some way. This can appear along a continuum from angry words to violent behavior.

9. Manipulation:

In some relationships people use shame as a weapon. One person may call the other names, trying to make that person feel inadequate. This is one way to get power over another. The worse the other person feels, the more control one has over them. If both people in a relationship use shame as a weapon, it can perpetuate itself into a cycle from which neither can break free. Either one will use shame to belittle the other. This causes the one shamed to lash out and shame the other. This then becomes a cycle where both parties feel hurt and continue to lash out at the other in order to get control and revenge. Such relationships can spiral out of control, with neither person able to get out of the cycle without outside help.

10. Deteriorating Self-Image:

Here are examples of the sort of negative beliefs to which people experiencing SBA internalize, which reduces self-image.

- I am no good.
- I am not good enough.
- I am an outsider, I do not belong.
- I am not lovable.
- I should never have been born.

11. Shame-Based Anger Short-Term Strategy (STS):

A) Be sensitive to the anger cues. If you are alert to the cues, you can move from the situation. At a minimum, it can trigger the other short-term strategies from perception to calming.
B) Step away from the situation (or the Wookie), LEAP.
C) Perception: If you begin to process self-deprecating thoughts, you need to develop a counter argument to each negative self-image attack. Use the optimism skills from sessions I through III.
D) Perspective:

- What is the situation?
- Why has the anger cue come up?
- How does it impact the SBA?
- Is it sufficient to become angry?

    E) Calming: diaphragmatic breathing. If appropriate, speak to yourself in a calming voice. Consider voicing your counter arguments.

    F) Calm Communication: If available and applicable, invite the other(s) involved to express their issues without interruption. Do this with the understanding that you (the SBA) will be granted the same courtesy.

12. Shame-Based Anger Long-Term Strategy (LTS):

Some of the short-term strategies apply, as indicated below:

    A) Continue to trigger the counter argument when self-deprecating thoughts occur. The goal is to first trigger counter arguments. Eventually the need to internalize the anger situation, rather than evaluate it as an external situation, will diminish.

    B) Where applicable, use the Win/Win to No Deal as a resolution strategy to mitigate a protracted anger episode.

    C) In regard to triggers, perspective is used to determine the real weight of the trigger. When a trigger is encountered, begin the process of evaluating it in the form of counter arguments.

    D) Use cues as a trigger/prompt to take a walk, go outside, or sit outside; then close your eyes and just listen. Focus on identifying all the words or sounds you hear.

    E) Continue with the optimism and self-forgiveness week 3 exercises.

13. Shame-Based Anger Affirmation:

I am a good person, worthy of love and respect.
I love and respect others.
I appreciate all of the relationships in my life,
seeing the beauty and perfection in all things.

14. Moral Values:

Respect: If we were able to respect ourselves and others, many of the conflicts of our daily lives would diminish or disappear. "Never pay back evil for evil to anyone. Respect what is right in the sight of all men. If possible, so far as it depends on you, be at peace with all men" (Romans 12:17-18).

<u>You are Valued</u>: Know that we are valued, the "slings and arrows of outrageous fortune", mentioned by Shakespeare, are a little more tolerable and life becomes easier. "Since you are precious in my sight, since you are honored and I love you, I will give other men in your place and other people in exchange for your life" (Isaiah 43:4).

<u>God Loves You</u>: "We have come to know and have believed the love which God has for us. God is love, and the one who abides in love abides in God, and God abides in him" (1 John 4:16). Keep the following words of comfort in mind. "God is our refuge and strength, a very present help in trouble" (Psalms 46:1).

15. Homework:

- Continue to use the Anger Control Today (ACT), recording events as outlined in session 1, emailing observations to the counselor.
- Begin the week 2 self-control skill training homework.
- Continue using an Anger Affirmation as part of the overall anger management plan.

16. Yoga:

Run through the seated yoga stretches, following the instructions in part 16 of session II. In both this and the breathing exercise, include music that fits the anger management program criteria.

17. Diaphragmatic Breathing:

Perform the breathing exercise as outlined in part 17 of session II.

Chapter 9

Session VII: Deliberate Anger

"He who is slow to anger has great understanding, but he who is quick-tempered exalts folly" (Proverbs 14:29).

1. Update and Review:

    A) Review with members any questions they may have regarding the previous session on shame-based anger. Members should have their Anger Control Today (ACT) file available, updating it when appropriate.

    B) Self-Control Week 2 Review:

A level of complexity was added to the assignment from week 1. This exercise involved applying self-control, at will, on a simple task. Instead of a daily or routine task, the reward was contingent on completing a self-assigned task. An example could have been calling a parent or loved one with whom you have not spoken in a while.

2. Anger Control Today (ACT):

    A) Every life event is potentially a springboard to better understanding and growth. This course attempts to retrain thinking to see the positive associated with seemingly negative events. It is important to make the focus of these anger control reviews about how members faced and overcame situations that triggered their anger. At this point in the course, certain patterns of behavior may begin to repeat themselves. The beginning of the course primarily focused on techniques for managing anger. When negative behavior patterns repeat, we should ask the question of why, rather than blame someone or something else. What is not working in the overall treatment strategy? What needs changing? The anger control review should lean toward solution-oriented discussions in the remaining six sessions.

B) Conduct an Anger Control Review following the instructions in part 11 of session I. Continue with the proceeding questions:

- Highest number on the scale?
- Anger Categories?
- Anger Cues?
- Triggering event and Antecedent Behaviors?
- Strategies used to control the anger?

3. Session Overview:

- Positive Psychology: Self-Control Week 3
- Discuss the Deliberate Anger Style

4. Positive Psychology:

A) Self-Control: Week 3/Scenario 1:

Have members read the scenario 1-pt 1. After members have answered the proceeding questions, pass out scenario 1-pt 2. Wait until everyone is finished before going on to the out-of-class exercise.

B) Self-Control: Week 3/Out-of-Class Exercise 3:

Give members the out-of-class exercise. Answer any questions they may have regarding the assignment. Screen any questions that are best answered at the debriefing in session VIII.

5. Deliberate Anger:

Some people deliberately appear to be angry in order to manipulate others. In this regard, deliberate anger shares this quality with both sneaky anger and anger avoidance. Such individuals attempt manipulation through intimidation, blame, and sometimes guilt. The cause of the anger is either internal, such as the desire to impose one's will upon another, or the cause is external. This depends upon the individual's manipulative goals and how others react to them. As with any manipulation, there is some sort of deception. The anger usually begins contrived. There is a point where continuing forward with escalation of anger is easier than admitting deception or defeat. The person may actually become angry during this escalation.

6. Benefits of Deliberate Anger:

A person who feels they can manipulate others to get what they want is operating under a dangerous set of morals. These "flexible" morals provide immediate benefits and payoffs when other people capitulate or back down. This is the main reason people use this anger style. It can be broken down into the following four reasons: [25]

A) Power: Deliberate anger can be used to make others comply with your demands. It is a form of control, both of situations and of one's own emotions. Such individuals typically feel more comfortable and in control using anger than expressing other emotions. In some cases people use deliberate anger to abuse others psychologically and physically. When psychological abuse is resisted, the anger must then escalate. Such individuals will "externalize" the anger by blaming the victim for the escalation. This then excuses them for initiating violent actions.

B) Image: Some individuals display an unhealthy projection of the ego. They may project an image of power, declaring they are in control. Such displays are often reinforced by the compliance of others. They are positively reinforced (enjoy) manipulating others with anger. Some seek approval or respect from others, by acting this way.

C) Distance: This is a form of security. By appearing that one could "go off at any moment", or that they are "volatile", they create distance between themselves and others. It can be a way to create emotional distance, to keep from getting too close to others. The message being sent is, "I am dangerous, keep your distance, give me space."

D) Emotional Avoidance: This refers to other emotions one feels uncomfortable expressing or experiencing. Deliberate anger is a controlled and pseudo-emotional state. In this case deliberate anger is not used to manipulate others, but to avoid uncomfortable emotions.

7. Negative Consequences of Deliberate Anger:

Short-Term Costs:

- Though you may gain some sort of control, you create ill will and bad feelings. Therein lies the danger, since not everyone is weaker than you.
- Frequently we have stated that the nervous system does not distinguish between a perceived and an experienced event. Thinking about anger will create measurable changes in your brain and in your body. Pretending to be angry can activate your Sympathetic Nervous System (SNS). Your heart rate increases, blood vessels dilate, epinephrine injects into your blood stream from the adrenals, and cortisol is released. Before you realize it, you are actually angry, threatening to act out what was initially only pretend. The danger then is escalation to the point of explosion.

Long-Term Costs:

- Your relationships with others are damaged. Physical violence, dishonesty, and manipulation all contribute to causing others to avoid and resent you. In the business world, healthier people are not going to deal with you. You will miss out on relationships, business opportunities and untold life opportunities, all because of your manipulative use of anger. This may also place you into a position where others retaliate against you.
- The use of this strategy may result in the individual not handling genuine anger situations appropriately. This may cause a range of other problems.
- A person using this anger style to avoid other emotions is likely hampering their emotional growth.

8. Overcoming Deliberate Anger:

We recommend that those who use this style of anger consider the following:

A) What you are doing is manipulative, and may also be directly harming others.
B) Anger styles such as this have limited positive value, with the real chance of damaging your relationships.
C) If you are able to incorporate the morals described in part 12 of this chapter, you will live a happier life, free from the dangers and consequences of deliberate anger.

Session VII: Deliberate Anger

9. Deliberate Anger Short-Term Strategy (STS):

The goal of this strategy is breaking the cycle of this behavior pattern.

A) Activate this strategy when you are first aware of anger or a desire to implement deliberate anger.
B) Pause at the start of a disagreement. Stop speaking for a count of five. Gather your thoughts.
C) Listen to the other individual, inviting that person to speak without any interruption.
D) In the absence of a life-threatening situation, if a decision needs to be made, ask the other individual(s) to postpone the decision. Use this time to give thought to the other person's goals and comments.
E) If a decision need not be made and you are not listening to the other individual, LEAP into a time-out. Acknowledge the other individual(s) before walking away.

10. Deliberate Anger Long-Term Strategy (LTS):

A) Write down the last three times you used deliberate anger. Answer the following questions:

   - How did you do it?
   - Who did you affect by it?
   - What did you gain by using deliberate anger?
   - What were the short-term payoffs and consequences?
   - What are the long-term consequences of using this anger style?

B) Develop skills of compromise. Begin by relinquishing control of small situations and the associated decisions. First listen to the other person, calmly express your side, and leave the decision to the other person.
C) Listen to the other person's issues if the disagreement is not decision oriented. Consider the weight of the disagreement. Ask the other person if the disagreement is worth arguing.
D) Solicit support from others. Approach the people close to you and willing to help you make changes, such as a significant other. Explain to them that when you are angry, you use deliberate anger. Let them know that you are committed to changing this behavior pattern. Ask them to support this change. When you disagree in the future,

they should listen to your views in a balanced manner and express their disagreement calmly. Both parties should have the goal of compromise.

E) Record the antecedent situations to determine if there are other emotions you are not permitting yourself to feel. Examples include sadness, grief, fear, and joy. Look for the potential benefits of experiencing those avoided emotions. Record those benefits.

F) If you use a support system, make them aware that changing this pattern of behavior can take time, and that you may backslide. If you do, record the situation and what you were unable to apply of the STS or LTS. Adjust the strategies as necessary to account for any relapses in behavior. Stay motivated and dedicated to change.

11. Deliberate Anger Affirmation:

I will not harm others by word or deed;
I will listen to others first.
I acknowledge my true feelings when dealing with others.
Keeping perspective I acknowledge not all things are worth fighting.
I am willing to compromise and include others in solutions.

12. Moral Values:

Respect: This value was covered in session VI, mostly in regard to the self. This same value is relevant in regard to others and deliberate anger. Those who manipulate others to get what they want, rather than dealing genuinely with people, are being disrespectful. It is a form of deliberate selfishness. "Never pay back evil for evil to anyone. Respect what is right in the sight of all men. If possible, so far as it depends on you, be at peace with all men" (Romans 12:17-18).

Do Not Harm Others (Ahimsa): There are many scriptures regarding not harming others. Here are a few examples, "Do not devise harm against your neighbor, while he lives securely beside you. Do not contend with a man without cause, if he had done you no harm. Do not envy a man of violence and do not choose any of his ways" (Proverbs 4:29-31). "In everything, therefore, treat people the same way you want them to treat you, for this is the law and the Prophets" (Matthew 7:12).

Honesty and Truthfulness: Honest people avoid some of the problems that deceitful people face. By always sticking to the truth or saying nothing at all, but always doing what you believe to be right, you will avoid a great deal of life's tests and troubles. Honesty and true conduct go hand in hand. Honesty and truth apply toward both oneself and others. Ask yourself, "Am I really angry?", "Am I avoiding other emotions?", "Am I using anger to hurt others and/or feel in control?", "Am I truthfully trying to change?".

Actions that you are not willing to admit committing, are probably not right to do. If you are using anger to manipulate others, then chances are, you keep this secret. This is a sign to you that the given action (manipulation or deception) is wrong. The Bible speaks often of this subject. "O' Lord, who may abide in your tent? Who may dwell on your holy hill? (answer) He who walks in integrity, and works righteousness, and speaks truth in his heart. He does not slander with his tongue, nor does evil to his neighbor, nor takes up reproach against his friend" (Psalms 15:1-3).

Keep Promises/Vows: The biblical advice is to not make any oaths. "Again, you have heard that the ancients were told, 'You shall not make false vows, but fulfill your vows to the Lord.' But I say to you, make no oath at all, either by heaven, for it is the throne of God, or by earth, for it is the footstool of His feet..." (Matthew 5:33-35). But, a person should be good to their word. If you are committed to change, you will put forth effort. Accept that we are all fallible. If you backslide, promise yourself to continue working. If you are going to make a promise, show the fortitude to stand by it. People will only deal with you in as far as they know you are true to your word. "From you come my praise in the great assembly; I shall pay my vows before those who fear Him" (Psalms 22:25).

Here are what some other religious books state regarding these same values:

The Yoga Sutras 2:30-31 state: "The yamas are nonviolence, truthfulness, refrainment from stealing, celibacy, and renunciation of (unnecessary) possessions. These are considered the great vow. They are not exempted by one's class, place, time or circumstance. They are universal."[26]

The Qur'an states: "And make not Allah's (name) an excuse in your oaths, against doing good, or acting rightly, or making peace between persons, for Allah is one who hears and knows all things. Allah will not call you to account for thoughtlessness in your oaths, but for the intention in your hearts, and he is oft-forgiving, most forbearing" (2:224-225).

13. Homework:

- Continue using the Anger Control Today (ACT), recording events as outlined in session 1, emailing observations to the counselor.
- Complete the Self-Control week 3 out of class exercise.
- Continue using an Anger Affirmation as part of the overall anger management plan.

14. Yoga:

Run through the seated yoga stretches, following the instructions in part 16 of session II. In both this and the breathing exercise, include music that fits the anger management program criteria outlined in part 15 of session II.

15. Diaphragmatic Breathing:

Perform the breathing exercise as outlined in part 17 of session II.

Chapter 10

Session VIII: Excitatory Anger

"In all things moderation" - Socrates
(Addendum): "including moderation"

1. Update and Review:

A) Review with members any questions they may have regarding the previous session on Deliberate Anger. Members should have their Anger Control Today (ACT) file available, updating it when appropriate.

B) Self-Control Debriefing:

Most anger escalates because one or both of the individuals either lose control or fail to stop a negative pattern (cognitive or behavioral) from continuing. The exercises were simple, achievable demonstrations that increased in difficulty. Confirming that you have the ability to apply self-control, raises your self-control confidence. Even in the middle of an anger episode, that will translate into greater confidence, which will allow you to successfully self-control.

The passive-aggressive (PA) person will automatically default to focusing their lack of cooperation by projecting it at the person with whom they are angry. When a situation occurs where you are projecting, as a LTS you should instead honestly state "I have not fully embraced this task and may not have given it my best effort". This is difficult to do in the beginning. It is easier by starting with statements such as, "Let me work on that project (or task) a little more". In this statement you are not making any direct admissions, but you have interrupted the usual cycle of projecting your anger onto your target. By performing this step you resist your normal PA pattern and exhibit self-control.

For explosive anger styles, the initial demonstration of self-control might simply be walking away from the situation (or event) in the beginning. By exercising this level of self-control, you expand your levels of self-control. For both types of anger categories, you should record the number of anger episodes and the number of times you were able to exert self-control over yourself, interrupting the behavior cycle or pattern.

Count the number of short-term strategies you use. Also look at how broadly they are each applied. Ask yourself questions such as:

- How many anger episodes do I have in a week?
- Do I mostly rely on one or two strategies?
- Am I able to apply strategies in broad or diverse ways?
- Is there a pattern to my anger episodes? Are they every day, every other day, at night, etc?

See if you are versatile in your strategy use. For example, if you only use the LEAP time-out, you might be reinforcing an anger avoidance pattern.

2. Anger Control Today:

Conduct an Anger Control Review following the instructions in part 11 of session I. Continue with the proceeding questions:

- Highest number on the scale?
- Anger Categories?
- Anger Cues?
- Triggering Event and Antecedent Behaviors?
- Strategies used to control the anger?

3. Session Overview:

- Discuss the Excitatory Anger Style

Session VIII: Excitatory Anger

4. Positive Psychology:

Empathy is one of the Virtue/Strength/Skills (VSS) of this program. Like optimism or self-control, it applies to a wide range of anger management strategies. How can you know when and how to apply a given strategy if you cannot understand your own emotions and the emotions of others? Improving the ability to recognize emotional cues and states has direct application to many of the techniques thus far implemented. Empathy has acknowledgment of other's worth at its core. It is critical to good communication and active listening

  A) Empathy: Week 1/Scenario 1:

Have members read scenario 1-pt 1 found in Appendix E. After members have answered the 6 related questions, pass out scenario 1-pt 2. Wait until everyone is finished before going on to the out-of-class exercise.

  B) Empathy: week 1/Out-of-Class Exercise A & B:

Give members out of class exercises A & B. Answer any questions they may have regarding the assignments. Screen any questions that are best answered at the debriefing in session X.

5. Excitatory Anger:

People develop anger styles because of a broad spectrum of factors, including genetics, life experiences, and developed behavioral schemas. Most people experience anger as an unpleasant or negative emotion. Excitatory anger is unique in that those who exhibit this style do so for the good feeling that it brings them. This is akin to a "rush" or a "high". Some research suggests that this is accompanied by the release of adrenaline during emotionally heightened situations. Anger provides a unique opportunity because most people can voluntarily escalate and intensify it. In some people this results in the release of "feel good" neurotransmitters in the brain such as dopamine and serotonin. The activation of these chemicals is strongly related to emotional parts of the brain. Thus one can feel both physically and emotionally elevated from experiencing anger. They could also experience the relaxation cycle similar to an athlete successfully completing an event; the calm after the storm.

The pleasure excitatory anger addicts experience after a rage episode is obvious and apparent. Such people seek our rather than avoid anger opportunities. Every anger invitation is a chance to get another "fix". For them, feeling good is more important than anger. Anger is just a means, and anger invitations are really just an excuse.

6. Benefits of Excitatory Anger:

Excitatory anger can be viewed as a type of addiction. Like all of the anger styles in this book, excitatory anger does have some perceived benefits. This is especially true in the early stages, where excitatory anger can be:

- Cathartic/A Great Feeling: People who exhibit this anger style generally express feeling emotionally cleansed after an anger episode. They may also just "feel good".
- Stimulating: Being angry can make one feel clear, sharp, and alive. It has a way of drawing one into the present moment.
- Intense: Some people like the intensity that anger brings to their relationships. For those in intimate relationships, their intense feelings can become further entangled as they may engage in physical intimacy after an argument; thus confusing intensity and intimacy.

7. Negative Consequences of Excitatory Anger:

- Dependency: The need to get high is fundamental to any addiction. A combination of physical, psychological, and emotional dependencies can drive this. Addicts almost always tell themselves, "I am in control and can stop at any time". A person is usually long past the point of quitting on their own before they realize they cannot stop. This is especially true of psychological addictions, such as excitatory anger.
- Increased Tolerance: Due to the psychological concept of the hedonistic treadmill, over time it takes more of a given stimulus to produce an equal amount of response. This phenomena is more commonly defined as tolerance. Over time it takes more intense anger to get the same adrenaline rush. Longer and more intense anger episodes carry increased risk of harm to self, others, and an increased risk of negative social consequences.
- Inability to Stop: Because of the addictive nature of excitatory anger, such people run the risk of finding themselves in a dangerous situation where they want to engage rather than back down. After a certain point in a confrontation, they may find it

impossible to back down. This sort of addictive behavior results in a loss of control. Loss of control reduces decision making options, leading one to making poor decisions.

- <u>Emotional Avoidance</u>: A person may cause themselves severe emotional harm, replacing other appropriate emotions with anger. In situations where a normal emotional response is expected, they may react with anger. This can lead to the development of maladaptive or emotional reactive-state disorders.

8. Signs of Excitatory Anger:

Below are some of the behaviors that indicate the presence of excitatory anger:

1. A feeling of confrontation, "looking for a fight".
2. Interpreting generally benign situations as negative in order to drive them toward anger.
3. Feeling the desire or need to get high from anger.
4. Developing a feeling of accomplishment after an anger episode.
5. Needing more anger for the same feeling.
6. Confusing intimacy for intensity in personal relationships.
7. Pushing oneself to "losing it".
8. Raging out of control.
9. Before a conflict, feeling anticipatory excitement as something positive.

Because of excitatory anger's addictive style, there are also associated thinking errors:

- <u>Rationalizing</u>: This involves explaining why we got angry and why we keep doing it. Any excuse besides the real one, getting high, will suffice. Examples include, "I just had a bad day", or "If you would not...(insert any excuse), I would not get so angry with you".
- <u>Minimizing</u>: People will say things such as, "That argument was not that bad", or "You really are blowing the incident out of proportion". These excuses are designed to make a problem appear less important than it actually is. It is an attempt to draw attention away from the real problem, addiction and/or emotional masking.
- <u>Denying</u>: Denial is used to convince oneself other people or innocuous events are the cause of the anger and thus the problem. For example: if you get arrested after a fight and ignore what your family says and then say, "it was the other guy's fault." Such

people will also deny they even have an anger problem. They might even perceive bringing their addiction to their attention as an anger invitation.

- Perception Distortion: Perceiving situations as negative in order to create opportunities for anger.

9. Patterns of Addictive Behavior:

Generally speaking the characteristics of these individuals appear as follows:

- The person engages their addiction generally on a regular basis unless an event is so intense they withdraw from the behavior for a time. If they were alcoholics people might refer to them as "functional alcoholics". Some addicts even claim they function better high than sober. A person in an excitatory anger maintenance pattern would regularly be on the alert for anger invitations. They may appear pessimistic, complaining, and sarcastic, but frequently in a "dark mood". Some days they are angry, other days they find an excuse to get their anger fix. A person in such an anger pattern appears negative most of the time.
- For various reasons, some people get angry less frequently. They might be happier people, or perhaps they are in the beginning stages of moving into a pattern of always seeking anger invitations. Such people are still exhibiting excitatory anger, they just get angry less often. On some days their positive qualities may appear so clearly that people might feel they are dealing with two separate people. When they fully engage an anger episode, they can possibly carry on for hours or longer. Such an addiction pattern is dangerous because of the potentially extreme nature of their behavior when they are binging.

In total, these signs, thinking errors, and addictive behavioral patterns are indicators of excitatory anger. In some cases, a person may share these indicators with other anger styles such as habitual hostility. Excitatory anger addicts can incorporate other anger styles, such as moral anger in order to justify their cravings for conflict.

10. Overcoming Excitatory Anger:

Before discussing strategies for dealing with this anger style, let us review anger invitations from session II. Learning to be aware of and decline anger invitations is an important component of managing excitatory anger. Review with members the examples of anger invitations. Such examples may include: a person asking you, "What are you looking at?", or "What's your problem?". They may include behaviors such as a person bumping into you, someone giving a derogatory gesture at a traffic stop, or making a pass at your significant other.

Anger addicts look to turn anger invitations into rage invitations. This can be especially satisfying since many anger invitations can appear to be the fault of the person who extended them. Thus they can satisfy their addiction and still appear to be in the right. The apparently negative situations that trigger these rages are not the root of the problem. Einstein quoted, "Within adversity lies opportunity". It is in one's best interest to learn to take problems and turn them into opportunities. Anger addicts instead take anger invitations (opportunities) and turn them into problems (rage episodes). Learning to recognize and deal with anger invitations is one of the tools necessary for executing the short and long-term strategies regarding excitatory anger.

11. Excitatory Anger Short-term Strategy (STS):

As with any form of explosive anger, breaking the immediate cycle of the trigger to emotional and physical outburst is key. Replacing negative thoughts and behavioral patterns with healthier responses is done as follows:

1. Step away from the situation. If it involves other people, politely explain that you will be back. This begins the adjustment phase of the LEAP strategy.
2. You need to associate your possible outburst with the potential negatives. Example: would the situation have been dangerous had you engaged your anger? Were you going to hurt someone or something? Would there have been negative consequences?
3. Gain perspective on the situation to determine if anger was an appropriate response. Example: did the person intentionally bump into you or was it an accident? Are you feeling depressed or anxious, and not really angry?
4. Calmly review the situation. Where appropriate, talk to yourself in an unhurried, calm voice.
5. Once you feel your emotions decelerating, return to the situation. If it involves others, calmly invite them to express their issues. Maintain perspective.

There will be situations where anger is the appropriate reaction. When appropriate anger involves discussion with others, rather than elongate or intensify the conflict, focus on problem solving and active listening. As part of this strategy, review and familiarize yourself with Calm Talk from session V part 12B. Also review the Win/Win to No Deal strategy outlined in session II part 9.

12. Excitatory Anger Long-Term Strategy (LTS):

The goal of the LTS is for the member to extend the time between anger episodes and to appropriately implement the listed behavioral and cognitive strategies. The challenge for this strategy involves 3 principle areas:

1. <u>Cognitive Modification</u>: Changing reactionary thought patterns.
2. <u>Behavioral Replacement Therapy</u>: Replacing the perceived behavioral (physical) benefits of an anger episode with healthy behaviors.
3. <u>Introspective Perception</u>: Addressing emotions that have been masked using anger as the default behavior. What was the strong emotion you were feeling prior to becoming angry?

A) Cognitive Modification: This is driven by a person's ability to understand events as they happen. Record the triggers of any anger event as well as the thoughts prior to the escalation of the event. This is much like the instructions regarding the anger meter review that each member conducts.

- What are the associated triggers?
- What were your first thoughts associated with the trigger?
- What was your emotional state?
- Were you anticipating the anger episode? If so, was the anticipation giving you positive feelings?

The focus of this exercise is to "think" through the immediate rush of thoughts to the point they replace the desire to extend or intensify anger episodes.

Desensitization Techniques are used to gradually put a situation causing fear of or desire for anger to a minimal and manageable state. This will be particularly effective when the member is masking other emotions with anger. Identify the avoided emotion by using the introspective perception exercise. The counselor should create mental scenarios for members where a common anger trigger is used. They may give an insult that makes the member angry, such as implying they are overweight. The counselor then asks the member to list a positive trait they possess or give a counter argument. Over time the counselor can add more negative elements to the scenario and guide the member into addressing the avoided emotion. Eventually the avoided emotion is accepted as part of the normal spectrum of emotions for that member.

B) Behavior Replacement Therapy: For Excitatory Anger one must relate to the physical reward of anger. Members should identify physical activities which give them similar results. Maybe they can exercise at a gym, go running, swimming, or rock climb in an indoor facility. Maybe the act of taking an aggressive walk will suffice. These types of physical activities can produce the same highs and emotional dumping of an Excitatory Anger episode without the negative consequences.

C) Introspective Perspective: When the member begins to experience their desire for anger, they need to begin their thinking exercises. This includes both the short-term strategy and the Cognitive Modification of the long-term strategy. Is this a genuine situation that warrants anger? i.e. A coworker insulted the member's spouse. Does the situation need an immediate response, such as in a disagreement?

The ability to take oneself through these steps involves using self-control. Each time the member is using these thought patterns they are:

a) Exhibiting Self-control (and)
b) Engaging in Behavioral Replacement Therapy

13. Excitatory Anger Affirmation:

I keep events in perspective, looking for the good in them.
I have the power to choose my behavior and how I act toward others.
My intensity is only expressed through positive emotions, such as love and joy.
I face my emotions and feel good in healthy ways.

14. Moral Values:

Calmness / Gentleness: This is the ability to remain calm when life presents chaos. If you picture in your mind's eye the ideal wise person, invariably it coincides with images of someone peaceful and tranquil. People who can remain calm and avoid unnecessary conflicts often deal more effectively with many of life's problems. Scripture says, "Cease from anger and forsake wrath; do not fret, it leads only to evil doing" (Psalm 37:8). "The Lord's bond-servant must not be quarrelsome, but be gentle unto all men, apt to teach, patient when wronged" (2

Timothy 2:24). "Let your gentle spirit be known to all men" (Philippians 4:5). Members may refer to Session V, part 12B on Communicating Calmly.

Temperance / Self-control: Self-control is a component of all anger strategies, and thus influential in dealing with all anger styles, including Excitatory Anger. "Now for this very reason also, applying all diligence, in your faith supply moral excellence, and in your moral excellence, knowledge, and in your knowledge, self-control, and in your self-control, perseverance, and in your perseverance, godliness," (2 Peter 1:5-6). "But the fruit of the Spirit is love, joy, peace, patience, kindness, goodness, faithfulness, gentleness, self-control; against such things there is no law" (Galatians 5:22-23).

Moderation: As was mentioned in the opening quote, all things in moderation. Moderation is one of the components of temperance, a virtue that counteracts addictive behavior patterns such as Excitatory Anger.

15. Homework:

- Continue using the Anger Control Today (ACT), recording events as outlined in session 1, emailing observations to the counselor.
- Begin the week 1 Empathy out of class exercises A & B.
- Continue using an Anger Affirmation as part of the overall anger management plan.

16. Yoga

Run through the seated yoga stretches, following the instructions in part 16 of session II. In both this and the breathing exercise, include music that fits the anger management program criteria outlined in part 15 of session II.

17. Diaphragmatic Breathing:

Perform the breathing exercise as outlined in part 17 of session II.

Chapter 11

Session IX:
Resentment/Hate

"Resentment is like drinking poison and hoping it will kill your enemies." - Nelson Mandela

1. Update and Review:

   A) Review with members any questions they may have regarding the previous session, Excitatory Anger. Members should have their Anger Control Today (ACT) file available, updating it when appropriate.
   B) Empathy: Week 1 Review:

Return the completed week 1 scenarios to the members. Review the week 1 out-of-class exercise, both A & B. Ensure the instructions are well understood, as members will complete the week 2 scenarios in this session. Questions regarding the psychology of the empathy instruments should be answered in the next session, during the debriefing.

2. Anger Control Today (ACT):

Conduct an Anger Control Review following the instructions in part 11 of session I. Continue with the proceeding questions:

   • Highest number on the scale?
   • Anger Categories?

- Anger Cues?
- Triggering Event and Antecedent Behaviors?
- Strategies used to control the anger?

3. Session Overview:

- Positive Psychology: Continue developing the Virtue/Strength/Skill (VSS) of empathy.
- Discuss the resentment/hate anger style.

4. Positive Psychology:

A) Empathy week 2/scenario 2, pt. 1 & 2:

Provide members scenario 2, pt. 1, located in Appendix E. After members have completed all of the assigned questions, distribute scenario 2, pt. 2. Wait until everyone is finished before going on to the out of class exercises.

B) Empathy week 2/Out-of-Class Exercises A & B:

Give members the out of class exercises A & B. These are the same exercises assigned the previous week. Since they are the same exercises, there should be minimal questions regarding their completion. The empathy debriefing will occur in the next session.

5. Resentment/Hate (R/H):

Of the four chronic anger styles R/H is the first one introduced into the 12 sessions. Forgiveness is an intricate component of the R/H anger style treatment and can take a significant amount of time to develop. It is incorporated in this session's moral values. In the next session, forgiveness skill development exercises will begin. This allows, before the course's end, group leaders and counselors sufficient time to engage in individual therapy regarding resentment/ hatred. As explained in the introduction, chronic anger styles can be viewed as characteristics of other anger styles. There are two general ways hatred presents itself. First it can be directed inward. This generally manifests as anger turned inward. This was discussed in session IV and included a self-forgiveness skill development exercise that also improved self-image and enhanced the long-term strategy for anger turned inward. The second way for R/H to manifest is toward others. The rest of this chapter is dedicated to dealing with that.

Session IX: Resentment/Hate

Hatred is generally defined as a deep and intense loathing toward someone. The cause can be real or perceived. The harm can be toward the hater or toward someone or something for whom the hater has an emotional attachment, such as a spouse, child, or parent. When hatred is directed toward others, it can become a consuming force, dominating all of our thoughts. Resentment is a less intense feeling that can easily move toward hate, especially with those who have a previous pattern of hating. People who are in the throes of this powerful emotion are sometimes capable of doing things that they would not normally do. If the hater allows the hatred to build, they may feel the need to take more overt action. They may harm themselves for not actively protecting themselves or others, or harm the one who is the focus of their anger. Haters plot revenge, and in extreme cases can kill. Hatred tends to be enduring. Hate can become an ongoing problem where a person is trapped in their thoughts and emotions, unable to let go of the wrongs done to them. For those who suffer from chronic hatred, it can consume them, leaving them emotionally stuck and ultimately unhappy in life.

6. How Resentment and Hatred Develop:

There are three main components to the formation of hatred.

A) First, a person must in some way feel harmed or injured either mentally, physically, or emotionally. Resentment can build as a result of some sort of harm. Usually the more severe the harm, the more intense the reaction. As resentment continues building or if the harm is grievous enough, hatred can form.

B) Second, a person must continue to dwell on the hurt or wrong done to them. Haters think about negative past situations. If a situation persists, the hate can intensify. If a person caused the hater significant harm or emotional pain, the hater may encounter triggers reminding them of the harm. They may continue reliving those negative events, thereby developing a cycle of hate.

C) Third, a person must believe they were unjustly harmed. This may be accompanied by feelings of helplessness, inadequacy, or injustice. This is related to a victim mentality. Feeling internally weak can be degrading and painful. To compensate for the feelings of injustice and helplessness, thoughts of revenge can form. Revenge is an unhealthy way for a person to try balancing the scales and regaining their power. Remember Herman Melville's book *Moby Dick*, where Captain Ahab said, "Out of the heart of hell I stab at thee, for hate's spite I spit at thee"? Few recall that Captain Ahab was last seen tethered to the whale he so loathed, sinking beneath the waves; his hate having consumed and destroyed him.

7. Benefits of Resentment/Hatred:

Hate has very few constructive outcomes, but like all anger styles, R/H has some positive value. Hate can serve as a healthy reaction to a real injury to oneself or someone for whom they care. The feeling of hate may qualify one's reaction. This may be accompanied by related emotions, such as sadness or remorse. Exhibiting these related emotions is a healthy expression of hate.

Resentments may form to tell us the people and things we should avoid. If someone or something is causing us pain, we should reassess our relationship with them. That uncomfortable feeling is a warning that we should take a closer look. Perhaps we need to address a problem, or leave a relationship that is harmful. Resenting someone because of a real harm indicates that a resolution is needed. Meeting and discussing with the person can open the door to resolution, forgiveness, and the release of negative feelings.

8. Negative Consequences of Resentment/Hatred:

As early as the first session, we explained that anger can lead to many social, emotional, and physical problems. Hatred can also manifest in other anger styles. It can lead to revenge and destructive behaviors. Those who hate carry the heavy burden of negative feelings such as resentment, inadequacy, helplessness, or guilt. Ruminating on negative feelings is unproductive, unhealthy, and can lead to depression or violence. Hate can compromise the immune system, raise blood pressure, cause the heart rate to spike, and release stress hormones such as cortisol. Cortisol and similar hormones only exacerbate people's anger issues. Ultimately hatred harms the hater, but hatred can be overcome. Letting go of hatred is a conscious choice and a learned skill that leads one toward emotional freedom.

9. Overcoming Resentment/Hatred (For Group Leaders & Counselors):

Resolving Resentment and Hatred involves cognitive visualization and the application of real life situations. The ultimate goal is resolution. Empathy and forgiveness may be a part of that final stage. This may include the assignment of the negative feelings to some other outcome, such as in the judicial example. The strategies below incorporate these points.

Session IX: Resentment/Hate

10. Resentment/Hate Short-term Strategy (STS):

As with other short-term strategies the immediate issue is addressing concerns that my result in the harming of oneself or others. If the hater has formed a plan to harm others they need to perform the following:

1. Visualize the consequences of seeking vengeance. Example: Besides harming the target individual, does the action ultimately harm your life?
2. Focus on a positive future for yourself. Create a list of accomplishments and experiences you will enjoy in the future.
3. Name the injury. Bring the harm to light. Is it ruling you? By writing the injury on a piece of paper and destroying it, some or all of the resentment/hate will be released.
4. Plan and participate in a positive activity. Exercise, go to the movies with a friend, prepare a meal.
5. If possible and safe to do, discuss the issue with the "other" individual. Actively listen to what they say. As part of this strategy, review and familiarize yourself with Calm Talk in session V part 12B. Also review the Win/Win to No Deal strategy outlined in session II part 9.

11. Resentment/Hate Long-Term Strategy (LTS):

The focus of this strategy is forgiveness. Because of the severity of the harm, there are situations where forgiveness may seem impossible.

- If it is possible to forgive the individual, contact them and tell you forgive them. While doing this in person is the ideal way to communicate forgiveness, it may not be possible if the person has caused great harm.
- If the judicial system was involved in dispensing justice, permit yourself to release your burden at the time of conviction or sentencing. Equate the release of anger with the justice.
- Other forms of long-term strategies previously reviewed may apply based on the individual and the situation. Refer to the Group Leader or an individual counselor to help determine which strategies would be effective.
- If the previous strategies do not help to develop forgiveness, refer to Appendix F for additional methods for developing this skill as well as outside resources for helping with forgiveness.

12. Resentment/Hatred Affirmation:

I treat myself and others with kindness.
I have the strength to forgive myself and others.
Forgiveness sets me free.
Free from the past, I embrace a life of love and happiness

13. Moral Values:

<u>Forgiveness:</u>

Mahatma Gandhi said, "The weak can never forgive. Forgiveness is the attribute of the strong." Martin Luther said, "Forgiveness is pure happiness". Besides having many benefits to the forgiver, it is a moral value taught by the five largest world religions, Christianity, Islam, Buddhism, Judaism, and Hinduism.

"Be kind to one another, tender-hearted, forgiving each other, just as God in Christ also has forgiven you" (Ephesians 4:32).

"For this reason I say to you, her sins, which are many, have been forgiven, for she loved much; but he who is forgiven little, loves little" (Luke 7:47).

"For if you forgive others their transgressions, your heavenly Father will also forgive you. But if you do not forgive others, then your Father will not forgive your transgressions" (Matthew 6:14-15).

"Hold to Forgiveness; command what is right; but turn away from the ignorant" (Quran, Surah 7:199).

<u>Do not take Vengeance:</u>

Vengeance can both personally and spiritually harm the one seeking it. The Law of Compensation ensures that the harm we cause others will be paid back in full. "Do not be deceived, God is not mocked, for whatever a man sows, this he will also reap" (Galatians 6:7).

"You shall not take vengeance, nor bear any grudge against the sons of your people, but you shall love your neighbor as yourself; I am the Lord" (Leviticus 19:18). Though originally written in the context of Judaism, Christians take this verse to mean any neighbor, regardless of their beliefs.

"Never take your own revenge, beloved, but leave room for the wrath of God, for it is written, 'Vengeance is Mine, I will repay,' says the Lord" (Romans 12:19).

<u>Do not Hate</u>:

"The one who says he is in the Light and yet hates his brother is in the darkness until now. The one who loves his brother abides in the Light and there is no cause for stumbling in him" (1 John 2:9-10).

"Hatred stirs up strife, but love covers all transgressions" (Proverbs 10:12).

14. Homework:

- Continue using the Anger Control Today (ACT), recording events as outlined in session 1, emailing observations to the counselor.
- Begin the week 2 Empathy skill training homework.
- Continue using an Anger Affirmation as part of the overall anger management plan.

15. Yoga:

Run through the seated yoga stretches, following the instructions in part 16 of session II. In both this and the breathing exercise, include music that fits the anger management program criteria outlined in part 15 of session II.

16. Diaphragmatic Breathing:

Perform the breathing exercise as outlined in part 17 of session II.

Chapter 12

Session X: Habitual Hostility AND Fear-Based Anger

"Your beliefs become your thoughts. Your thoughts become your words. Your words become your actions. Your actions become your habits. Your habits become your values. Your values become your destiny." - Mahatma Gandhi

1. Update and Review:

A) Review with members any questions they may have regarding the previous session, Resentment/Hate. Members should have Anger Control Today (ACT) file available, updating it when appropriate.

B) Empathy Debriefing:

Have the members who are willing, share their recordings and insights from this exercise.

C) Debriefing: The purpose of the empathy exercises was to develop two key, fundamental skills.

1. Improve skills related to looking at and correctly interpreting physical cues that express emotion.

2. Help work through recalling situations where you felt the same as other people in similar situations.

Session X: Habitual Hostility AND Fear-Based Anger

Each scenario added a level of complexity in identifying the emotional cues of others. The methods varied from direct observation, to direct interaction. As each scenario added levels of complexity, it was intended for you to improve your ability to identify similar situations from your own experiences.

The first out-of-class exercise was designed to improve the identification of physical cues in real life situations. The level of difficulty increased in these scenarios because there was only direct observation. Such situations have potentially more variables than in a controlled scenario, and so the exercise was designed to push your observational skills.

The second out-of-class exercise was to speak to someone in a low challenge situation about a real life experience. This was to involve an emotionally charged anger situation. This provided you with practice in:

- Calmly asking about a sensitive issue.
- Listening to someone else's side.
- Considering how another person interprets a situation.
- Considering how their past experiences can assist them to understand and empathize.
- Using empathy to help resolve situations.

In the future, when you are directly involved in less aggressive (non-physical) disputes, use the skills in the Q & A portion of out-of-class exercise B. You should combine this with the active listening modeled in the resolution of the church scenario.

2. Anger Control Today (ACT):

Conduct an Anger Control Review following the instructions in part 11 of session I. Continue with the proceeding questions:

- Highest number on the scale?
- Anger Categories?
- Anger Cues?
- Triggering Event and Antecedent Behaviors?
- Strategies used to control the anger?

3. Session Overview:

- Positive Psychology: Begin the exercises on forgiveness.
- Discuss the Habitual Hostility Anger Style (Habitual Anger).
- Discuss Fear-Based Anger.

4. Positive Psychology:

A) Forgiveness of Others:

Forgiveness provides many benefits to the forgiver.

- Just visualizing forgiving causes people to experience less negative emotions, such as anger and sadness, compared to people who imagine the hurt or grudge they held.[27]
- Forgiveness provides less anger, less stress, more optimism, and better reported health.[28]
- Forgiveness helps sustain relationships by preventing the formation of permanent wedges and lasting hurts.
- People who forgive are more likely to donate time and money to charity, and tend to feel socially connected.[29]
- Those who learn to forgive, can free themselves from feelings of hatred and anger.
- Since the benefits of forgiveness go to the forgiver, it is a gift to yourself.

B) Forgiveness: week 1/Scenarios 1 & 2 (part 1 of each):

Provide members the appropriate scenario, located in Appendix F. Have members answer all of the appropriate questions. Collect the data, giving it to the group leaders. If your program provides for individual therapy, these various positive psychology instruments are beneficial in assessing each individual member's progress, level of participation, and skill in that particular area.

C) Forgiveness: Week 1/Out-of-Class Exercise 1 (3 parts):

Give members the appropriate exercise, located in Appendix F. Between now and the next session, members are to apply the questions to any real life situations they have previously or are currently experiencing. Do not use extreme scenarios, such as the hypothetical example of the harm of one's family. Describe the situation in two or three sentences, briefly answering the provided three-part questions.

Notes to group leaders: Detailed analysis for the participants and counselor, the counselor analysis for additional consideration, and the forgiveness instruments are found in Appendix F. Skill development summaries for the members are also provided in each applicable session.

5. Fear-Based Anger and Habitual Anger:

Both of these anger styles are usually developed as characteristics of anger styles discussed in previous sessions. Inward anger and explosive anger styles may include both of the components and the elemental components of Fear-Based and Habitual Anger. In this session, both styles are discussed with these perspectives in mind.

6. Fear-Based Anger:

It can be argued that all anger has some basis in fear. With paranoia, fear can become a certainty. In human history, fear and anger have been necessary for our survival. But what if every person was suspicious, every lover a cheater, every banker dishonest, and everybody was trying to get something from us? If our suspicions and fears cause us to see threats in all things, paranoia has set in. If we then react to it through projection, accusations, and anger, we have the makings of the fear-based anger style.

Paranoia can be the product of anger or it can be the cause. If a person is exhibiting inward anger, they may become paranoid. They may believe certain people are, in some way, trying to hurt them, when in fact they are not. They might believe a co-worker assigned to work with them, or supervisor who has verbally reprimanded them, is out to get them.

When a person is paranoid, it may illicit anger. They may become angry because they have few people they can trust, or the anger may be related to something they fear. Such stress may cause resentment and more anger. Paranoia can therefore server as a trigger or a characteristic of anger. It is more commonly intertwined with inward anger, such as with the passive aggressive (PA) person. It can combine with explosive anger styles where the culmination of paranoid stress is the trigger.

7. How Paranoia Develops:

Fear-based anger and associated paranoia stem from four sub-components: jealously, greed, envy, and insecurity.

1. Jealousy generally involves a relationship, or a perceived relationship with one or both of the following components.
   - The jealous person may fear their significant other has stronger feelings for someone else.
   - The jealous person may fear losing the relationship to a perceived competitor or adversary. This may be a real fear. Example, your significant other appears attracted to another person.

2. Greed does not simply focus on the accumulation of wealth or power. It may also focus on insufficient time to acquire things or the fear of losing those things already acquired.

3. Envy involves the perception that someone else possesses something the envious person does not feel they can develop or acquire. This may include traits, material objects, or intangibles, such as love. They may feel cheated and have issues of self-worth.

4. Insecurity deals directly with one's self-inadequacies. The perceived inability to achieve or to succeed are examples of what an insecure person may feel. Most of these components relate to poor self-image. The consequences of the stress created by these unresolved issues cross the various anger styles, not just paranoia.

8. Benefits of Fear-Based Anger:

The fight or flight response is tied to fear. Earlier peoples needed these responses to the environment in order to survive. While the need to run from hungry lions has substantially decreased, our built in fear response has not. The fight or flight response continues to operate, held in reserve for perceived dangers. Sometimes, when the fear is real, fight or flight is an appropriate response.

9. Negative Consequences of Fear-Based Anger:

The continual struggle with the components of jealousy, greed, envy and insecurity can lead to developing a range of disorders. Anger follows as a result of the overwhelming stress of these four emotions. In small, intermittent doses, these emotions are experienced by most people. Most people can manage these feelings if they have a reasonably healthy self-image. Otherwise, all of these can be very destructive to a person's emotional state, especially if the stress is persistent.

10. Habitual Hostility:

In this pattern, harsh behavior results in a person frequently becoming angry. The habitual hostility becomes a mechanism to respond to a wide range of situations. It can be an extension of anger turned inward or deliberate anger. It generally manifests itself as a result of persistent poor self-image or from the development of the need for experiencing anger. Habitually angry individuals will respond to a broad range of situations with anger as a strategy.

11. Benefits of Habitual Hostility:

In situations, such as a fight, where a person is facing real harm if they fail to act, anger is an appropriate reaction. Beyond this, habitual hostility has very few, if any, real benefits.

12. Negative Consequences of Habitual Hostility:

Habitual anger is extremely destructive. The consequences include poor social interactions, the physical effects of prolonged stress, and prolonged negative moods. All of the negative consequences of inward and explosive anger styles may also apply.

13. Fear-Based Anger and Habitual Hostility Short-Term Strategy (STS):

These anger styles are based upon components that are generally characteristics of other anger styles. Fear-based anger (paranoia) can be considered a characteristic of anger turned inward and shame-based anger, covered in sessions IV and VI. Habitual hostility can be considered a characteristic of sudden anger and deliberate anger, covered in sessions V and VII. Use the corresponding short-term strategies outlined in those chapters.

14. Fear-Based Anger and Habitual Hostility Long-Term Strategy (LTS):

The applicable long-term strategies are applied in the same manner as the above short-term strategies.

15. Fear-Based and Habitual Anger Affirmation:

I resolve my fear and negative emotions.
I change the things I can.
Within reason, I accept the things that seem unchangeable.
I resolve problems without hostility.
I replace negative thoughts with positive counter arguments.
I focus on the present moment.

16. Moral Values:

Remove Fear: Fear can be a component of many anger styles. By learning to overcome our fears, we can live happier lives. Religious faith can help to counteract some of the negative effects of fear. "Even though I walk through the valley of the shadow of death, I fear no evil, for you are with me; Your rod and Your staff, they comfort me" (Psalm 23:4). "There is no fear in love; but perfect love casts out fear, because fear involves punishment, and the one who fears is not perfected in love" (1 John 4:18).

Avoid Jealousy: Learning to trust some people and living life without jealousy can improve social connections and how much we enjoy life. Because of the root fear, jealous feelings diminish our relationships. Learn to let fears go and become free. "For jealousy enrages a man, and he will not spare in the day of vengeance" (Proverbs 6:34).

Avoid Greed: One of the mysteries of life is that people who have a mindset of plenty tend to have plenty. By contrast, people who are greedy, tend never to have enough. Learn to share and give. Abandon fear and greed: "Then he said to them, 'Beware, and be on your guard against every form of greed; for not even when one has an abundance does his life consist of his possessions'" (Luke 12:15).

Avoid Envy: Many of the world's religions teach one to abandon envy. They know that envy leads to darker emotions and actions. Abandon envy while it is still small. "You lust and do not have; so you commit murder. You are envious and cannot obtain; so you fight and quarrel. You do not have because you do not ask. You ask and do not receive, because you ask with wrong motives, so that you spend it on your pleasures" (James 4:2-3).

Perseverance: Simply stated, perseverance is continuing on in the face of adversity. In the context of anger management, it is the will to continue with treatment strategies when faced with back-sliding. Winston Churchill had a famous speech where he said, "Never, never, never, never, give up". In Romans 5:3-5 it says, "but we also exult in our tribulations, knowing that tribulation brings about perseverance; and perseverance, proven character; and proven character, hope; and hope does not disappoint, because the love of God has been poured out within our hearts through the Holy Spirit who was given to us".

17. Homework:

- Continue using the Anger Control Today (ACT), as outlined in session I, emailing observations to the counselor.
- Begin the week 1 Forgiveness of Others skill training homework.
- Continue using an Anger Affirmation as part of your overall anger management plan.

18. Yoga:

Run through the seated yoga stretches, following the instructions in part 16 of session II. In both this and the breathing exercise, include music that fits the anger management program criteria, outlined in part 15 of session II.

19. Diaphragmatic Breathing:

Perform the breathing exercise as outlined in part 17 of session II.

Chapter 13

Session XI: Moral Anger

"People are to be taken in very small doses." - Ralph Waldo Emerson

1. Update and Review:

   A) Review with members any questions they have regarding the previous session, Habitual Hostility and Fear-based Anger. Members should have their Anger Control Today (ACT) file available, updating it when appropriate.
   B) Forgiveness: Week 1/Review:

The first week involved two hypothetical scenarios. Through those scenarios, we developed three foundational skills.

   1. Our first focus was on non-harmful resolution. The second set of questions taught that the benefits of forgiveness go to oneself.
   2. The two scenarios taught the potential steps to resolve a situation vs. the destructive planning involved in resentment.
   3. Severe situations, such as the murder scenario, do not have the same burden of resolution. Such situations can be delegated to an appropriate outside force. In such situations, control of punishment is given to the legal authorities.

The out of class homework involved applying skills applied in the in-class scenarios to real life situations.

Session XI: Moral Anger

2. Anger Control Today (ACT):

Conduct an Anger Control Review. If time is available in this session, group leaders may discuss these events in more detail and/or with more members. Conduct the review, following the instructions in part 11 of session I. Continue with the proceeding questions:

- The highest number achieved on the scale?
- Anger Categories?
- Anger Cues?
- Triggering Event and Antecedent Behaviors?
- Strategies used to the control the anger?

3. Session Overview:

- Discuss Moral Anger
- VSS Forgiveness Week 2

4. Positive Psychology:

   A) Forgiveness: week 2/Scenarios 1 & 2 (part 2 of each):

Give the members the second part of the two scenarios, located in Appendix F. Additional information is added to both scenarios. After reading the scenarios, have members complete the corresponding questions.

   B) Forgiveness: week 2/Out-of-Class Exercise 2:

Give members the out-of-class exercise 2, located in Appendix F. Answer any questions they may have regarding completing the task. Screen any questions regarding the test's psychology. Reserve those for the forgiveness debriefing in session XII.

5. Moral Anger:

This is also called righteous indignation or righteous wrath. It is the anger that is triggered when a person's values or beliefs are threatened. Things such as politics, religion, and personal honor can also trigger it. It can manifest as explosive anger or as inward anger. Moral anger has two components:

1. A sense of moral superiority; the idea that one side is "right" and the other is "wrong".
2. Using this moral superiority to justify feeling angry or taking aggressive actions against others.

Moral anger can be used by individuals to justify their behavior. Nations sometimes use it to lead their people to war. There are countless examples of moral anger throughout history, and many examples today.

6. Benefits of Moral Anger:

Such anger can motivate social reform and political change. Moral anger can be the energy that motivates people to help or protect others. It can take the form of outrage that motivates people to do something positive or improve the world in some way.

7. Negative Consequences of Moral Anger:

More people have probably been harmed in events related to moral anger than to all other types of anger combined. History often uses moral certainty to motivate large groups of people to kill one another. Examples where moral anger was involved include the following: The Crusades in 1099, the Russian Revolution, Germany's 40 year's war, the ideological conflict between Sunnis and Shiites, and the current conflict with ISIS.

8. Overcoming Moral Anger:

The previous lessons on empathy, self-control and active listening are essential tools in dealing with moral anger. Empathy and active listening help one to understand another's point of view. Self-control helps one to consistently apply the anger management strategies. As a brief review, ask members to explain how empathy, self-control, and active listening may help with moral anger.

9. Moral Anger Short-Term Strategy (STS):

Moral anger can be exhibited as inward or explosive anger styles. Use the short-term strategies in session IV and VI if the trigger is inward. For explosive anger, use the strategies from sessions V and VII. In addition to the short-term strategies of both of these styles, the person triggered by moral anger needs to have an immediate means of defusing the anger episode. This is to accept that, as an exercise of self-control, the situation can be reduced if the concept of No Deal (Win/Win to No Deal) is employed. Listening before communicating is key. No Deal in this case means not to convert others to your viewpoint, but to instead empathize with them.

10. Moral Anger Long-Term Strategy (LTS):

The person triggered by moral anger must be prepared to achieve resolutions by accepting the possibility that No Deal may be the answer. Rarely does a person who feels they are on the moral "high ground" concede that ground. Just as rare is the fact, that despite this perception of high ground, do they persuade many people to their views. Use the following combined techniques to manage moral anger long-term:

- Seek resolution: Win/Win to No Deal as described in the STS.
- Develop points of common ground. Combine this with developing counter arguments that are positive to the points you disagree with of theirs. If the argument is with yourself, the counter arguments relate to an alternate perspective.
- Active Listening: Ask open-ended questions. This is to understand WITHOUT judgment, not to debate or persuade.
- Diaphragmatic Breathing: Calm yourself. This will calm your reactions.
- Instead of LEAPing alone, invite the other person to speak with you while you walk together.

11. Strategy Review:

At this point all of the short and long-term strategies have been taught. Take this time to review the members' most commonly used strategies for the anger styles they have identified. Answer any questions members may have regarding any strategy. Aside from the style specific strategies, the most common short-term strategies are as follows:

- Time-out (LEAP)
- Active Listening
- Win/Win to No Deal
- Perspective
- Diaphragmatic Breathing
- Calm Communication

Aside from the style specific strategies, the most common long-term strategies are as follows:

- Behavioral or Cognitive Modification Plan
- VSS Training
- Using the ACT plan
- Yoga/Exercise

12. Empathy:

First discussed in session VIII, empathy is a VSS relevant to many anger styles. A primary component to active listening, it is incorporated in most anger style STS, including moral anger. The following exercise is designed to help improve empathy and listening skills.

Carry a "memory object", aka a mnemonic device. This could be a polished stone, a piece of jewelry, or a coin necklace. The idea is to have something small and easily accessible that you carry with you. Whenever you are in a conversation and remember to work on listening and empathy, touch or hold your "memory object". This is a reminder to listen to the other person while they talk, to not interrupt them. When they pause from talking, let go of the memory object. Ask questions designed to help you understand what the other person thinks and feels. Once you have asked your question, touch or hold the memory object. This will remind you not to interrupt as you listen patiently to what the other person is expressing. Understand what it must be like to experience life from their viewpoint. Once you have truly understood a person, you may find they are much more understanding of your needs and point of view.

13. Moral Anger Positive Affirmation:

I listen to others, considering their viewpoint.
I try to understand how others feel.
I am adaptable in my thinking.
I only engage my anger when absolutely necessary.

14. Moral Values:

Humility: Healthy humility involves appreciating the worth in others while still retaining a sense of one's own self-worth.

Session XI: Moral Anger

"Pride goes before destruction, and a haughty spirit before stumbling. It is better to be humble in spirit with the lowly than to divide the spoil with the proud" (Proverbs 16:18-19).

Discretion: This involves knowing when to engage in a worthy cause or fight, and when to walk away. Remember the beginning of the serenity prayer? "God, grant me the serenity to accept the things I cannot change, the courage to change the things I can, and the wisdom to know the difference."

Ecclesiastes 3:1-2 says, "There is an appointed time for everything. And there is a time for every event under heaven. A time to give birth and a time to die; a time to plant and a time to uproot what is planted." Knowing the proper time of things or when to leave things as they are, involves using discretion.

15. Homework:

- Continue using the Anger Control Today (ACT), as outlined in session I, emailing the observations to the counselor.
- Complete the Forgiveness Out of Class Exercise 2.
- Continue using an Anger Affirmation as part of your overall anger management plan.

16. Yoga:

Run through the seated yoga stretches, following the instructions in part 16 of session II. In both this and the breathing exercise, include music that fits the anger management program criteria as outlined in part 15 of session II.

17. Diaphragmatic Breathing:

Perform the breathing exercise as outlined in part 17 of session II.

Chapter 14

Session XII: Concluding Session

"Sometimes a cigar is just a cigar." - Sigmund Freud

1. Update and Review:

A) Review with members any questions they may have regarding the previous session, Moral Anger. Members should have their Anger Control Today (ACT) file available, updating it when appropriate.

B) Forgiveness: Week 2: Review:

Members were to speak to someone with whom they had unresolved anger issues.

- Were they able to contact a person?
- Were they able to apply any of the resolution skill sets, such as listening?

2. Anger Control Today (ACT):

Conduct an Anger Control Review following the instructions in part 11 of session I. Continue with the proceeding questions:

- Highest number on the scale?
- Anger Categories?

Session XII: Concluding Session

- Anger Cues?
- Triggering Event and Antecedent Behaviors?
- Strategies used to control the anger?

3. Session Overview:

- Positive Psychology Final in-class exercise on forgiveness of others. Debriefing of all forgiveness of other's skill training.
- Summary of anger styles covered in each session by category, with examples of each category.
- Take Away: Exercises, review of strategies, ongoing VSS development.
- Q & A:
  - A) Anger Styles
  - B) Instruments for continual VSS development
  - C) Back Chaining and Back Sliding

- Final yoga stretches and Diaphragmatic Breathing Exercises.

4. Positive Psychology:

A) Forgiveness: Week 3 / In-Class Exercise:

Give the members the week 3 exercise, located in Appendix F. After completing the questions and collecting the answers, proceed to the debriefing.

B) Forgiveness Debriefing:

The Forgiveness of Others VSS training was designed to focus on forgiveness as a resolution and a benefit to both the forgiver and the one forgiven.

1) Analysis of Exercises / Week 1:

The first week involved two hypothetical scenarios. Through these scenarios we developed three foundational (VSS) skills. You should have learned the following:

- Non-harmful resolution is the first focus.
- The second set of questions that showed the benefits of forgiving others go to oneself.

- The potential steps to resolve a situation vs. the destructive planning of resentment.
- Severe situations, such as the murder scenario, do not have the same burden of resolution. Such situations can be delegated to an appropriate outside force (locus of control).

No interaction was necessary in order to apply the first six questions to a real life situation. The first step was for you to incorporate a resolution mindset to a negative situation (the first three questions). You were then asked to reevaluate the situation. This was an underlying reason for the separation of the first set from the second set of questions. The second set of questions were written to illustrate, to the person harmed, the possible negative, long-term ramifications for not forgiving.

2) Analysis of Expansion of Skills / Week 2:

The additional information was to cause you to work through the evaluation process.

A) In scenario 1, we added the part about the competitor's wife's health. It was not added as an excuse, but as a possible reason for their actions. There was no instruction provided as to whether the competitor's negative behavior was unusual or normal for them. The information was intended to:

- Elicit empathy.
- Develop optimism by suggesting that a resolution may be possible.
- Suggest that the competitor's actions might be forgivable.

The questions were slightly altered to suggest the unhealthy consequences for the person harmed.

B) Scenario 2 helped teach the following:

- Empathy. The murderer had a neurological disorder which may have influenced their behavior. This may have elicited some empathy despite the terrible outcome.
- One should relinquish part of the closure to the judicial process. This suggests transferring part of the resolution to an outside entity.
- The only person hurt by hatred is the victim. The questions focused on the issue of resolution and the importance of extinguishing hate. This is not necessarily done through forgiveness, but is accomplished by abandoning hate.

Session XII: Concluding Session

For ongoing VSS forgiveness development, continue the week 2/out-of-class exercise 2, located in Appendix F. There you will also find further suggested reading on the subject of forgiveness.

5. Review of Anger Styles:

It is important for members to note that, over the course of their lives, most people exhibit more than one anger style. The anger style a person exhibits most frequently is the first one addressed in managing anger.

A) Inward anger styles, such as passive aggressive (PA), share the following traits:

- The anger is not openly displayed.
- In most inward anger styles, other than PA, the person usually has some type of self-image issue. This dictates they are responsible for the anger episode.
- PA individuals use sabotage and undermining to vent their anger. They may have self-image issues that do not allow them to overtly express their anger.

B) Explosive anger styles usually require immediate responses because of the potential harm involved. Sudden or excitatory anger, like all of these anger styles, share a common set of issues:

- The anger is overt and readily displayed.
- The anger can deteriorate into violence.
- Most short-term strategies must include self-isolation.

C) Chronic anger styles, such as hate/resentment or fear-based anger, appear more likely as exaggerated characteristics of inward and explosive anger styles. Hate/resentment can be seen in PA as well as sudden anger. Fear-based anger is more readily associated with inward anger styles. Whether chronic anger styles are really characteristics of other anger styles or are actual anger styles is irrelevant. The real issue is, if these remain as active, unaddressed emotions, they are destructive to the person struggling with them and the people around them.

D) Moral Anger has been addressed separately from the other chronic anger styles. It is most likely expressed in PA, sudden anger, and excitatory anger. If you are expressing anger through a moral trigger, you may need to consider a No Deal (Win/Win to No Deal) or perspective training to reduce and control anger episodes. Sometimes walking away, agreeing to disagree, is the best solution. While moral anger is more likely a trigger of other anger styles, morality as a divider is particularly troubling. The current international crisis of terrorism is based on groups of individuals who believe they have a moral mandate to "punish" people of different beliefs and moral codes.

Throughout this program elements of morality have been incorporated. As indicated at the onset of this book, the need to include morals and ethics as a core component of effective anger management is critical to long-term success. Unfortunately, when the moral codes of people conflict, the individuals can utilize the trigger to justify anger. Under these circumstances, the need for effective short and long-term strategies is crucial. However, if the person is on a mission of morality, they may be using excitatory anger as a means of fueling anger episodes. In such circumstances, the person will not seek to employ any type of anger suppression strategy.

For this and other divisive triggers, such as differing philosophical or political views, effectively addressing them suggests a need for further study. Why would a terrorist want to calm down? What replacement emotions and behaviors provide an outlet for the expression of moral differences without causing harm to anyone?

6. Benefits of Anger Styles:

The benefits of the various anger styles may be real or perceived. In some cases, the style is an evolutionary response (fight or flight). In other cases the benefit is to the individual exhibiting the anger, such as deliberate anger to force people to see their views.

For inward anger styles the perceived benefit is one of control and socially acceptable behavior. The PA can use undermining without the need for overt displays of anger. The person with anger turned inward can avoid the conflict by taking responsibility for the episode. For explosive anger styles, the benefit may be the release of stress, the ability to intimidate others, or the enjoyment of the feelings of strong emotional expression. Sudden anger provides the person with an explosive release. Tension is gone. For excitatory anger, the individual enjoys the experience of anger. In both cases, these individuals exhibit the aura of "if you don't see it my way, I am ready to fight". This is usually intimidating to others who are less confrontational. Most people would rather agree with this type of person or avoid them.

Session XII: Concluding Session

7. Negative Consequences of Anger Styles:

Inward anger styles have the distinct disadvantage that they are usually more harmful to the person using those styles than to those around them. The PA undermining and resistance must be controlled within the individual. Most people will recognize the PA as uncooperative and somewhat antagonistic. For other inward styles, such as fear-based, the responsibility for the anger begins to affect their outward mood and emotional state.

Because of the overt expression of explosive anger styles, they tend to drive people away. Close relationships are placed in jeopardy and there is a real likelihood of someone eventually coming to harm.

8. Short-Term Strategies (STS):

The short-term strategies were designed to address the immediate episode of anger. Taking a time-out (LEAP) is the first reaction for explosive anger styles. By removing yourself from the conflict for a few minutes, it permits you to work on calming. You may then prepare to listen and respond constructively. For inward anger styles, other than PA, the first step is acquiring perspective. What is the role of the individual in the anger episode that is balanced? Effective listening is important. It is equally important to have the ability to engage the other party to hear you constructively.

PA's need to express their anger more constructively and openly. Rather than undermine, they need to acknowledge their behavior. Then they need to make an effort to "own" the task they are undermining.

For moral triggers, the issue must be understood if you are exhibiting the anger or if you are facing someone else who exhibits this anger. The first is for the person exhibiting this anger. If they have a moral trigger with inward anger, follow the PA strategy outlined in session III. Explosive anger would follow the sudden anger strategy. One important additional note is that the person with moral anger must be prepared to go to the No Deal (Win/Win to No Deal) resolution. People who assume moral high ground in an argument, whether necessary or not, do not tend to relinquish this ground. Unfortunately, as they are then morally superior, they tend to push people away rather than convert them to their way of thinking.

If you are facing someone who exhibits this anger, if the point of disagreement is a moral issue, you may never come to an agreement. See if there are other issues that need resolution. Otherwise, you may need to consider the No Deal option of the Win/Win to No Deal strategy.

9. Long-Term Strategies (LTS):

These strategies look toward developing a foundation for significantly eliminating the non-constructive anger. For explosive anger styles, the challenge is developing replacement behaviors to avert serious demonstrations of anger or harm and permit the person to reach a positive resolution. Calming, perspective, listening, optimism, and self-control are all significant skill players in this resolution effort.

For inward anger, including PA, the issue of perspective, constructive communication, and balanced expectations are all key to healthy expressions of anger. Optimism is certainly another primary element. The negative and counter argument optimism training would apply to both the situation and the other people involved. It would also apply to the inward anger individual, helping them apply appropriate counter arguments to themselves in order to gain a healthier perspective.

In the long run, those with moral anger triggers have to learn to accept that there are those with other perspectives. These perspectives include morality, even though it may not be what or at the level of their beliefs. It is quite difficult to live in a world of brotherly love if acceptance of differences is an issue.

10. Final Questions and Answers:

- Inward Anger
- Explosive Anger
- Short-term Strategies
- Long-term Strategies
- Positive Psychology, including VSS development
- Exercise and Relaxation Training

Session XII: Concluding Session

11. Ongoing Skill Expansion:

Throughout this program, participants worked on a broad range of skills. While this skill foundation is particularly effective in the management of anger, it can be applied to a wide range of emotional situations.

    A) The Positive Psychology Virtue/Strengths/Skills (VSS) enhanced through the program were:

1. Optimism
2. Self-Forgiveness
3. Self-Control
4. Empathy
5. Forgiveness of Others

The last exercise in each of these skill sets was designed to continue the development of these skills until they are the natural pattern of thinking (schema) of the participant. Confirm members have a blank final exercise and set of instructions for each of VSS skills. For example with optimism, in any situation where it seems easy to develop a list of negatives, develop a counter argument list. Using the framework of the last exercise of each skill training will ensure the continual refinement of that VSS. This includes the associated cognitive and behavioral responses.

The key skills for specific anger strategies include:

- Listening and effective communication
- Calming
- Perspective
- Perception

These are all core skills to managing anger and stress. "You get out what you put in" is the universal truth to any strategy or skill training. Practice is the key to everything someone wants to be good at.

    F) For exercise and calming, all participants should have mastered both stretching exercises from a chair and diaphragmatic breathing for relaxation. The concept of repeating these at the end of every session is to carry away a minimum of exercise and a solid technique for calming, diaphragmatic breathing. Ensure members have any instructions they may need to continue these beyond the class. Exercise such as yoga, pilates, swimming and weightlifting can go a long way toward giving the body the strength to fight stressful emotions, such as anger, without the physical need to resolve them through fighting. Fight the fight before it becomes a fight.

G) Music:

During the sessions, specific music was selected because of its benefits regarding anger. In the future, if members need some calming music, we encourage choosing it based upon the following criteria:

- Choose music with positive lyrics and themes, or without lyrics.
- Choose slow or moderate speed (tempo) music.
- Avoid fast music as it tends to excite people.
- Avoid negative, violent, or aggressive music.

Music, such as Jazz, Classical, Christian, Opera, Nature Sounds, Meditation, Love Songs, Hymns, Chants, Cultural such as Native or Aboriginal, Soft Rock, Easy Listening, and Instrumental such as Mandolin, Harp or Flute fit this criteria.

H) Nutrition:

Ensure members are aware of these basic dietary guidelines.

1. If possible, predominately eat whole foods such as nuts, grains, fruits, vegetables, fish, cheese, and meat.
2. Avoid the following: processed foods, refined sugar, tobacco, artificial sweeteners, saturated fats, and drugs.
3. Consume in moderation or caution: caffeine, alcohol, and table salt.
4. Follow the restrictions of your doctor, such as less meat and cheese for those with gout.
5. Get sufficient sleep. Lack of sleep can cause irritability and negatively affect health. For most adults sufficient sleep is about 6 to 8 hours per night.

Session XII: Concluding Session

12. Yoga, final session:

   A) Run through the seated yoga stretches, following the instructions in part 16 of session II. In both this and the breathing exercise, include music that fits the anger management program criteria.
   B) We have repeatedly stressed the importance of exercise for anger management. Encourage members to enroll or participant in some regular outside exercise class, such as yoga.

13. Diaphragmatic Breathing, final session:

Perform the breathing exercise as outlined in part 17 of session II.

Concluding Remarks:

We have come to the end of our journey and the beginning of another. Our members are not adolescent baboons that need a troop. They are skilled calming agents, first focused on their own calm and then that of others. Group members have developed a broad range of skills that effectively address anger. Beyond anger, these skills help to improve their overall quality of life.

The members travelled through 12 sessions of introspective investigation. They learned to understand how they expressed their anger and the cues to acknowledge the emotional change. They have identified their anger triggers and understand that not all anger invitations should be accepted. More importantly, they have learned how to decline those invitations without negative consequences, but the work does not end here.

Members need to continue honing their skills. Optimism skills not only provide a positive outlook on a situation, they provide a healthier perspective. Creating counter arguments to negatives create a perspective balance. Self-control then builds the ability to strike a healthy balance between the desire to react to negatives and developing counter arguments. Understanding how this affects others brings the value of empathy to the foreground.

Empathy provides the foundation to interpret other peoples' emotions. It also tunes members into cues they are displaying and the emotional signals they broadcast. Empathy then becomes the core foundation for forgiveness. Self-forgiveness provides the person with the chance to regain perspective and balance to center their emotional scale. Forgiveness of others is more easily achieved if one can forgive themselves. Remember, forgiveness benefits the forgiver.

We end this with our baboon troop of nice guys. Over 20 years later, the troop continues practicing social tolerance. The stress levels and subsequent harmful effects caused by anger are nearly absent. We do not suggest the true path to happiness and healthy anger is to model society after baboons. But like the baboons, we should keep reinforcing our skills. Our shared advantage is the desire to do better and continually build our skills for a healthier coexistence. This starts with the ability to live with ourselves and extends outward as we help one another to keep our skills sharp.

Appendix A

Anger Control Today (ACT)

This is the Anger Control Today (ACT) instrument. It is designed for members to use between sessions to track the following information regarding Anger Events:

1. Since the last session, record the highest number you reached on the anger scale (1-5). Also record the number of anger episodes. Since typically sessions are about 1 week apart, this should include a total of every anger episode you had since the last session.
2. The Anger Categories: Explosive Anger includes outburst and rage. Inward Anger is kept inside with little outward demonstration. There is also room included for specific anger styles.
3. Anger Triggers: These include the behaviors that lead up to the anger event (antecedent behaviors).
4. Anger Cues: These are what you feel, think, and experience that indicate you are becoming angry.
5. Short-term Strategies: These include the most common short-term strategies. Members should write in any appropriate strategy if they are working with a particular anger style.
6. Long-term Strategies: Follow the same format as the Short-Term Strategies.

Name:_____ Start Date:_____ End Date:_____
Session #_____

1. Anger Meter: 1 = no anger; 5 = feeling out of control
a) Highest number (1 to 5) you reached on the Anger Meter?_____
Number of Anger Episodes _____

2. Type(s) of Anger Experienced: Explosive Anger (Y/N)_____ Inward Anger (Y/N)_____
Specific Anger Style:_____, _____, _____, _____

3. Triggers (Check all applicable):

Person_____   Situation_____

Place_____   Words_____

Behavior/Action_____

Other_____ Other_____ Other_____

4. Anger Cues (Check all applicable):

Sweating_____ Hands Shaking_____ Increased Blood Pressure_____ Nausea_____

Headache_____ Hot Flashes_____ Nervous Ticks_____ Crying/Tears_____

Heart Palpitating_____ Screaming/Yelling_____ Cursing_____ Poor Concentration_____

Throwing Things_____ Punching_____ Depression_____ Anxiety_____ Fear_____

Violent Thoughts_____ Planning Harm to Self or Others_____ It is my fault_____

Other_____ Other_____ Other_____

5. Short-term Strategies (Check all applicable):

Time-out_____ Take a Walk_____ Breathing_____ Sit Quietly_____ Calming_____

Listening_____ Optimistic Exercise_____ Constructive Communication_____

Perspective/Perception_____

Other_____ Other_____ Other_____

6. Long-term Strategies (Check all applicable):

Win-Win to No Deal_____ Replacement Behavior_____ Behavioral Management_____

Desensitization_____ Perspective_____ Music_____ Empathy_____ Forgiveness_____

Exercise/Yoga_____ Meditation_____ Diet and Nutrition Therapy_____ Avoidance_____

Other_____ Other_____ Other_____

Comments:_____

_____

_____

Appendix B

Optimism:

Week 1: ICE Scenario1:   Name_____

You have to go to the grocery store. On your way to the store you come to a four-way stop. The only other car arrives at the same time you do and waves you to go first. You wave back. When you get to the grocery store parking lot, you arrive at a parking spot nearly the same time as another car who takes the space. You find a space further away. As you pass the car that parked ahead of you, you see a woman struggling to hold a baby bag while struggling to open a stroller. You hold the bag for her while she adjusts the stroller. You are in the store selecting items off of various shelves and someone bumps you with their cart. They apologize. You are at a checkout and the person behind you has two items and you have fifteen. You let them go ahead of you. You get to your car, load your groceries, and drive home.

List five positive actions (cues) in the scenario.
Positive Action List:

_____

_____

_____

_____

_____

Using the following scale, rate how difficult it was making the above list.
1 = very difficult; 2 = somewhat difficult; 3 = undecided; 4 = somewhat easy; 5 = very easy
Rating:_____

Week1: OOCE#1 (Positive Search):   Name_____

Each day, for the next 3 days, you are to list 5 positive actions you did for someone or someone did for you.
Ex: I helped someone carry some of their bags.

Positive Action List

	Day 1	Day 2	Day 3

Day 1 _____ Day 2 _____ Day 3 _____

_____ _____ _____

_____ _____ _____

_____ _____ _____

_____ _____ _____

Rate the level of difficulty in creating each day's list, based on the following scale:
1 = very difficult; 2 = somewhat difficult; 3 = undecided; 4 = somewhat easy; 5 = very easy

Day 1 Rating:_____ Day 2 Rating:_____ Day 3 Rating:_____

Week 2: ICE Scenario 2:   Name_____

You come home from a difficult day at work. Your spouse arrives home from their job a few minutes after you. They had agreed the night before they would cook dinner, but now they don't want to. You have your anger management meeting in an hour. You have been working on your explosive anger, which in the past has resulted in slapping your spouse. An argument erupts. You go from raised voices to shouting at each other. You grab a dinner plate and throw it against the wall. You then storm out of the house for a walk.

List 3 negative actions and 3 positive actions:

Possible Negatives	Possible Positives
_____	_____
_____	_____
_____	_____

Rate how difficult it was creating the above list based on the following scale:
1 = very difficult; 2 = somewhat difficult; 3 = undecided; 4 = somewhat easy; 5 = very easy

Rating:_____

Week 2: OOCE #2:   Name_____

List three (3) negative actions and three (3) positive actions you will take or observe over 3 of the days this week. Then rate how difficult it was developing the two lists each of the days.

Ex. You watch 2 people playing chess and they get into an argument. They are yelling, cursing at each other, and not listening (3 negatives). They do not get into a physical fight, they settle the dispute and start laughing, and they return to their game (3 positives).

Day 1 Negative   Day 2 Negative   Day 3 Negative
1st_____   _____   _____
2nd_____   _____   _____
3rd_____   _____   _____

Day 1 Positive   Day 2 Positive   Day 3 Positive
1st_____   _____   _____
2nd_____   _____   _____
3rd_____   _____   _____

For each day, rate how difficult it was to come up with both lists using the following scale:
1 = very difficult; 2 = somewhat difficult; 3 = undecided; 4 = somewhat easy; 5 = very easy
Day 1 Rating:_____   Day 2 Rating:_____   Day 3 Rating:_____

Week 3: ICE Scenario 3:   Name_____

You are driving your new car home from the dealership. Your spouse is in the passenger seat. You are going about 35 mph on a 4 lane, semi-residential road. There are fast-food restaurants and a couple of apartment buildings on both sides of the road. You are in the right-hand lane. A ball comes bouncing out onto the road form the parking lot of the apartment building on your right. A child chases after the ball and into the road. You slam on the brakes and swerve into the left lane. A car in the left lane hits your car in the front wheel panel and the front seam of your door. Your window shatters and you get some minor cuts. Your neck feels whiplashed. Your spouse bumps their head on the passenger door window. They receive a lump on their head and tell you they feel dizzy.

A. Rate the above situation based on the following scale:
1 = very negative; 2 = somewhat negative; 3 = undecided; 4 = somewhat positive; 5 = very positive
Rating:_____

B. List five negatives about the situation and then rate how difficult it was to come up with the list.

1 = very difficult; 2 = somewhat difficult; 3 = undecided; 4 = somewhat easy; 5 = very easy
Negatives:

1st_____

2nd_____

3rd_____

4th_____

5th_____

How Difficult? _____

C. List five counter arguments to each of the above negatives on your list.
Ex. Negative: I was cut with glass. Counter Argument: I was not seriously hurt.

Counter Arguments:

1st_____

2nd_____

3rd_____

4th_____

5th_____

Rate how difficult it was creating the counter arguments list using the same scale as for the negative list.
How Difficult? _____

D. Re-rate the overall scenario again based on the following scale:
1 = very negative; 2 = somewhat negative; 3 = undecided; 4 = somewhat positive; 5 = very positive
Rating:_____

Week 3: OOCE #3:   Name_____

Describe a dispute, disagreement, or argument (the event) with which you are either directly involved or observed. The description should be two or three written sentences. Complete the following ratings using the event as the scenario.

A. Rate the event based on the following scale:
1 = very negative; 2 = somewhat negative; 3 = undecided; 4 = somewhat positive; 5 = very positive
Rating: _____

B. List 5 negatives about the event. Then rate how difficult it was coming up with the list based on the following scale:
1 = very difficult; 2 = somewhat difficult; 3 = undecided; 4 = somewhat easy; 5 = very easy
Negatives:

1st_____

2nd_____

3rd_____

4th_____

5th_____

How Difficult? _____

C. List 5 counter arguments to each of the above negatives on your list.
Ex. Negative: The boss is a bastard. Counter Argument: The boss is having a bad day.
Counter Argument:

1st_____

2nd_____

3rd_____

4th_____

5th_____

Using the same scale as for the negative list, rate how difficult it was coming up with the counter argument list.

How Difficult? _____

D. Re-rate the event according to the following scale:
1 = very negative; 2 = somewhat negative; 3 = undecided; 4 = somewhat positive; 5 = very positive

Rating:_____

Week 1:

We are seeking to determine how difficult it is for the participants to create the lists. The participants scoring the list as very easy, are likely more optimistic. However, neither the scenario nor the out-of-class exercise is very difficult. We should expect to see scores slant toward optimistic. The scenario gives practice in developing a positive actions list. The out-of-class exercise expands upon that skill. It seeks to determine how comfortable they are with seeing positive actions, either by themselves or with someone else during a day.

Week 2:

You should expect to see some gradient differences. The ease to locate negatives in a situation should be relatively easy. This is the result of negative identifications assimilation, which is prevalent in most cultures. However, the positive listings should be expected to skew toward "not as easy". The greater the degree of separation, the stronger the pessimism; the closer, the more optimistic. Ex. The pessimist will rate the ease of the negative list at a 4 or a 5 but will rate the positive list at a 1 or 2.

The reason for the first week assignment and exercise being focused on generally positive situations looking for positives, is the training to seek positives first. For this skill to truly have a lasting effect, it would be better to run the exercise longer to determine if there is any significant change in the scoring.

In reviewing the week 2 exercises, you may ask the following questions:

- What were some of the negatives and positives of the situation?
- Was the second out-of-class exercise more difficult or was it about the same as the in-class scenario?
- Were the participants angry or frustrated with either list in their development?

Week 3:

The week 3 assignment and exercise was to assist participants to think in terms of:

1. Seeking the counter arguments in a generally negative situation.
2. Training their thinking to develop counter arguments (positives) to their negative lists.
3. Giving a better balanced perspective on negative situations, such as anger events.
4. Calmly assessing and weighing the elements of the event.

The expected outcomes:

1. The person scoring more toward the pessimistic side moving closer to neutral (undecided) to somewhat positive.
2. Optimistic people moving further toward optimistic scoring.
3. Optimistic people will re-rate the exercises and assignment as neutral or slightly more positive, after creating the counter argument list.
4. Pessimists will rate closer to neutral.

For long-term optimism skill development, the participants should continue performing exercise 3. In particular, focus on listing the core negatives of a situation and the counter arguments. One word of caution: People can fall into the habit of quickly listing the negatives, adding a quick counter argument, and then skipping over the importance of the counter argument. This essentially nullifies its effectiveness. Instead, while working on this skill, it is best to list all the primary negatives first, then list all the counter arguments.

Optimism Results and Measurements:

As with all the VSS skill developments, due to training duration, a core skill must be developed! Optimism is driven by a balanced perspective and the ability to see beyond the negatives of most situations. In this training the principle focus of the training begins with measuring the ability of participants to locate the positives of a situation. This progresses until we obtain the ultimate goal of the optimistic training: The development of counter arguments to real/perceived negatives of a situation.

The measurement of skills associated with the development of optimism is measured in terms of: low, moderate, and high. The goal is to raise everyone's optimism skill levels. The 3rd exercise is designed to also be the ongoing skill development and practice for the participants.

Week 3 Scenario and OOCE:

A and D are designed to reflect if the participant's perspective was affected by the use of Counter Argument skills. If they responded they rated the situation of either the scenario provided (the car accident), or a scenario they witnessed initially as a 1 or 2, followed by a 3 or higher for D after their counter arguments, their skill of applying constructive optimism was improved.

For B and C there are two combined ratings. First, the participants develop a list of negatives and rate the difficulty in developing the list. It is projected that most participants will find five negatives and rate the development of the list as somewhat or very easy. They are then asked to develop a counter argument for each negative they listed. If the optimism skill development is beginning to be applied successfully, they should be able to list five counter arguments. Assuming they can develop five counter arguments, this cognitive skill training can then be measured by the participant's response to how difficult the development was to complete.

If the training is effective, the participants should see a general up trend in this cognitive training, resulting in improved optimism as an applied skill.

Scoring for Optimism:

The scoring is rated on two categories, cues and the difficulty in creating those lists. Score the participants based on their lowest rating in either category. For instance 5 cues is scored as "3 pts. or High Optimism". A rating of 1 for "very difficult" scores as "1 point or Low Optimism". So a person who had 5 cues and rated it a "1" would score as Low Optimism.

Week 1: ICE Scenario 1:
High Optimism = 5 cues AND a rating above 3.
Moderate Optimism = 3-4 cues OR a rating of 3.
Low Optimism = Less than 3 cues, OR a rating less than 3.

Week 1: OOCE #1:
High Optimism = 5 actions/cues and a rating above 3.
Moderate Optimism = 3-4 actions/cues OR a rating of 3.
Low Optimism = Less than 3 actions/cues OR a rating less than 3.

Week 2: ICE Scenario 2:
High Optimism = 3 + 3 on cues and a rating above 3.
Moderate Optimism = No less than 2 cues per group AND a rating of 3 or 4.
Low Optimism = Less than 2 cues for either group OR a rating less than 3.

Note: If they misidentify a cue, it is not counted as an accurate cue.
Ex. "Taking a Walk" listed as a negative.

Week 2: OOCE #2:
Use the same parameters for scoring of OOCE #2 as the Week 2 ICE Scenario 2 above.

Week 3: ICE Scenario #3 and the OOCE #3:
Use the same scoring method for both the ICE and the OOCE.
Compare the ratings for parts A and D as follows:

High Optimism = A = 1 A = 1 A = 2 A = 2 A = 2 A = 3 A = 3 A = 4 A = 4 A = 5
             D = 5 D = 4 D = 3 D = 4 D = 5 D = 4 D = 5 D = 4 D = 5 D = 5

Moderate Optimism = A = 1 A = 1 A = 3 A = 4 A = 5
                 D = 2 D = 3 D = 3 D = 3 D = 4

Low Optimism = A = 1 A = 2 A = 2 A = 3 A = 3 A = 4 A = 4 A = 5
            D = 1 D = 1 D = 2 D = 2 D = 1 D = 1 D = 2 D = 3, 2, or 1

Week 3: ICE Scenario 3:

In this section we compare parts B and C. First, consider the number of negatives listed and the number of corresponding counters:

High Optimism = 5 negatives AND 5 related counters.

Moderate Optimism = 3 or 4 negatives OR 3 or 4 related counters OR a High Optimism score with one un-related counter argument.

Low Optimism = 2 or less negatives OR 2 or less related counters OR Moderate Optimism with one unrelated counter argument OR High Optimism with 2 or more unrelated counter arguments.

Then, look at the change in the difficulty in listing the five negatives (part B) versus listing the five counter arguments (part C). Score it using the following scale:

High Optimism (B,C) = 1,4 1,5 2,4 2,5 3,4 3,5 4,4 4,5 5,4 5,5

Moderate Optimism (B,C) = 1,3 2,3 3,3 4,3 5,3

Low Optimism (B,C) = 1,1 1,2 2,1 2,2 3,1 3,2 4,1 4,2 5,1 5,2

The final score for part B/C is determined by using the lower score between the number of negatives/counters listed, and the difficulty in generating those lists.

Exception to the scoring: If they score "High Optimism" in listing the negatives and counters AND they rate the difficulty as a 2/2 (which is Low Optimism), THEN score them as "Moderate Optimism".

Graphing: For OOCE: When there are multiple days of data reporting by the participants, graph each day. Then graph the mean for all three days. In cases where you have the ICE and OOCE on the same graph, graph them on separate lines. Then, connect all ICE and OOCE respectively.

Appendix C

Self-Forgiveness

Week 1: ICE Scenario 1:   Name_____

You observe two co-workers passing each other in the hallway. Both carry several folders and a cup of coffee. Worker #1 is reading a cover sheet on a file. Worker #2 is taking a drink of their coffee. They collide in the hallway was they pass, spilling their coffee on themselves. This initiates an argument.

Exercise A
Select one of the answers below:

Who is to blame for the argument?
1a) Worker #1 is to blame. _____
2a) Worker #2 is to blame. _____
3a) Both people are equally at fault. _____

Week 1: ICE Scenario 2:   Name_____

Put yourself in the role of worker #2. You are walking down the hallway drinking your cup of coffee (or other drink). Co-worker #1 and you collide and both of you spill your respective drinks on yourselves. For this exercise to be effective, it is very important that you close your eyes and visualize the scenario. Once you have walked 10-15 feet, visualize colliding into co-worker #1.

Exercise B
Select one of the answers below:

Who is to blame for the argument?
1b) Co-worker #1 is to blame. _____
2b) You are to blame. _____
3b) You both are equally at fault. _____

Look for two situations involving some level of blame. Examples may include the following:

- People in an argument
- A minor accident between two people
- Spilling a drink
- Tripping and falling
- Nearly falling, etc.

The situation may involve you. If it does, state that it does.

For any situation you observe or where you are involved, briefly describe the situation. If the situation involves you, you are person #1 (option 2). For situations involving two or more people you know, use only their first names. If you do not know them, use numbers or colors to label them, such as Mr. Green.

Select one of the options below for who is to blame:
1 = both are to blame; 2 = person #1 is to blame; 3 = person #2 is to blame

Situation #1
Description:

_____

_____

Selection: _____

Situation #2
Description:

_____

_____

Selection: _____

Week 2: ICE Scenario 3:   Name_____

You are at work. You are just returning to your desk/work station carrying a hot cup of tea. You are about to set your tea on your desk when someone calls your name. You turn to see who is calling. As you turn, you misplace your cup on the edge of your desk. Your cup falls, spilling the tea all over the floor.

Select one below for the above scenario. (mark only 1 answer):
1) I have no blame: _____
2) I share the blame: _____
3) I have all of the blame: _____

Week 2: ICE Scenario 4:   Name_____

You are at a friend's house watching a political show on TV. You and your friend have opposite political views. As the commentator presents a particularly sensitive and defensive issue, you make a statement to yourself how you do not agree with the commentator's comments. This is the opposite view of your friend. Your friend says that your view is wrong and you are misinformed. An argument starts. After about 15 minutes you decide to leave. The argument remains unresolved.

Select one below for the above scenario. (mark only 1 answer):
1) I am not to blame: _____
2) I share the blame: _____
3) I have all the blame: _____

Week 2: OOCE #2:   Name_____

You will record at least two incidents where you are involved in a disagreement or argument (event). You will write a brief description of each event and how many people, excluding yourself, are involved. Name each person with a color. Ex. You got into an argument with Mr. Green over a politician's views.

For each incident select one option from each of the following groups of statements:
Group A: Group B:
1) Both are to blame: _____   1) No one needs to be forgiven: _____
2) I am to blame: (person #1) _____   2) I need to be forgiven: _____
3) Person # 2 is to blame: _____   3) The other person(s) needs to be forgiven: _____

Incident #1 _____
_____
_____
_____

Incident #2 _____
_____
_____
_____

Evaluation Summary: Participant and Counselor

Self-forgiveness, when no forgiveness is required, is principally due to the assignment of blame. People with poor situational perspective and/or poor self-image may fall into a negative behavioral pattern of assigning self-blame. By improving participant's perceptions of the various arguments and their perspective on anger situations, they may not need to assign any blame.

In all of the scenarios and exercises, the primary focus is on the assignment of blame, which fosters guilt. The questions are designed to make participants ask, "Is blame really needed?" The act of self-forgiving is based on how self-blame and guilt are assigned by the participants. Wherever they assign self-blame (to themselves), they need to forgive themselves.

Week 1 / Analysis: Skill Sets:
The week 1 skills are designed to assist participants in learning that:

- There are gradients to blame that lead to guilt.
- Not all situations with a negative element require the assignment of blame.
- If some form of blame is to be assigned, it can be shared.

Week 2 / Analysis:
The skills of the first week are now expanded to look at a better perspective on a situation and to consider other ways of evaluating incidents which might normally require a negative assignment of blame.

The first set of ratings direct/minimize blame and the resulting potential for guilt.

The second set of scoring is to get a different perspective. By changing the assignments of the experience or situation, the participant is developing the ability to redirect the negative elements of a situation or incident. When individuals start developing a healthy self-image, self-forgiveness becomes possible. The scenarios are not meant to elicit great guilt or blame. The primary focus is appropriate assignment of blame, which fosters guilt. The next is, is blame really needed? By practicing the skill of healthy situational analysis, participants eliminate or minimize guilt, shame, and blame. The act of self-forgiving is based on how self-blame and guilt are assigned by the individual. Wherever the participants assigned some blame to themselves, they need to forgive themselves.

Consider the scoring differences between the need of the participant to rate levels of blame in the scenario to the person placing themselves into the scenario (week 1, pt. 2). What is being considered in the first set of scenarios is the weight the participants place on blame. In the second set of scenarios (week 2), the focus changes to both rating the need to assign blame and whether blame is substantial to the outcome of the scenario. By the end of week 2, the issue is whether blame even applies at all. This leads to perception of the individual in relationship to situations that produce anger or what might elicit poor self-image.

The first week out-of-class exercise looks at the assignment of blame in practical, real-life scenarios. In week two, the OOCE is expanded to give the participant the opportunity to recognize that forgiveness is a variable in resolution. However, the focal point is on where they assign healthy blame to themselves, and they recognize that self-forgiveness is still part of the resolution process.

Participants should continue applying the second week evaluation tools to situations where they assign themselves blame. In addition, they should practice the steps of self-forgiveness.

The following is the scoring for the self-forgiveness exercises.

The purpose of the first two in-class scenarios is to determine if the participant sees all situations requiring the assignment of blame. If blame is appropriately assigned, is the assignment likely rooted in a balanced manner (perspective)? First we have the analysis of the in-class scenarios for weeks 1 and 2.

Week 1, ICE Scenario 1:

The correct response should be either, neither person is to blame, or both are equally to blame.

Week 1, ICE Scenario 2:

Scenario 1 is then compared to scenario 2, which superimposes the participant as worker #2. In this case the concept is whether the assignment of blame is different, now that the participant is involved in the scenario. The change in assigning blame indicates if the participant tends to assign more responsibility to themselves in a situation. If so, and blame is the target variable, then the individual would require improved self-perspective to reduce the need for, and reduce the difficulty of, self-forgiveness. Various studies suggest that the more someone blames themselves for the actions of someone else's behavior or a situation, these individuals tend to have more difficulty self-forgiving.

Week 2, ICE Scenario 3:

In this scenario we are asking the participant for a healthy assignment of blame. The correct response is the participant is to blame for spilling the drink. There is no sharing of the blame. If the participant's response is that the person calling their name is, in part or in whole, sharing the blame, then they are seeking, more often than not, to inappropriately assign blame. This may suggest the person would use themselves as the default in assigning blame. This in turn would require some level of self-forgiveness where forgiveness should not be required.

Week 2, ICE Scenario 4:

This utilizes a more contentious scenario directly involving the participant. The topic of differing political views is used as the point of conflict. This is because political views can be a very polarizing topic. Many people, at one time or another, have found themselves in a conflict with an acquaintance, friend, or family member. There are other polarizing topics, such as religion, but these tend to be very highly emotionally charged discussions. The intensity of the emotion, especially when a core belief set (i.e. religious belief) is in contention, can result in a wide range of emotions infusing the situation. This emotional charge can skew data in defense of an intense belief system.

The correct response is that both individuals share the blame of the argument; meaning no one is to blame. Each enters the dispute with a predetermined difference of opinion. The fact that a comment was made aloud, does not negate the fact that the participant was sharing social time watching the TV. Such commentary is generally designed to stimulate discussion. The participant commenting aloud on the subject would be a normal behavioral reaction.

The scoring weight or blame points are as follows:

Week 1, ICE Scenario 1: (The correct answer is 3a of the scenario questions.)

Choice	* Weight / Blame Points
1a) Worker #1 is at fault	2
2a) Worker #2 is at fault	2
3a) Both people are at fault	0

Week 1, ICE Scenario 2: (The correct answer is 3b.)

Choice	* Weight / Blame Points
1b) Co-worker #1 is at fault	1
2b) You are at fault	2
3b) Both of you are at fault	0

Week 2, ICE Scenario 3: (The correct answer is 3.)

Choice	* Weight / Blame Points
1) I have no blame	2
2) I share the blame	1
3) I have all the blame	0

Week 2, ICE Scenario 4: (The correct answer is 2.)

Choice	* Weight / Blame Points
1) I am not to blame	2
2) I share the blame	0
3) I have all the blame	2

* The lower the weight score, the more accurate the perspective of blame assignment.

Week 1, OOCE #1:

The purpose of this exercise is to test the participants' ability to assign fault (blame) fairly, in a practical situation.

The participants were to find 2 incidences which involved some level of blame. These incidences are generally divided into two types of categories.

A) The first category is where both individuals share the blame.

B) The second category is where one person, based on their actions, is clearly to blame.

You will have to determine which category the situation describes in order to use the appropriate scale.

Their answers should be scored as follows:

Choice	Weight / Blame Points	
	Category A	Category B
1) both are to blame	0	1
2) person #1 is to blame	2	0 (the at-fault individual)
3) person #2 is to blame	2	2 (where clearly the wrong individual was blamed)

For Category B:
If blame is appropriately assigned, the score is 0.
If the wrong person is blamed, the score is 2.
If both parties are selected to blame, the score is 1.

Week 2, OOCE #2:

They were to record two incidences where they were involved in a disagreement. After describing the incident, they were to answer two sets of questions for each incident. The first set of questions, Group A, deals with the assignment of blame. The second set of questions, Group B, deals with the perceived need for Forgiveness. The first point to graph is the appropriate assignment of blame. This is scored in the same manner as OOCE #1 in week 1.

The second factor we are considering is the participant's willingness to SELF-forgive. IF they assign blame to themselves accurately, based on the scenario they describe, then the self-forgiveness points are zero (0). If they inappropriately assign blame to themselves, AND select choice 2 (I need to be forgiven), the score is 2. If they appropriately assign blame to person #2, but select themselves (I need to be forgiven), this is also scored as a 2.

Group A Group B
1) Both are to blame 1) No one needs to be forgiven
2) I am to blame (person #1) 2) I need to be forgiven
3) Person #2 was to blame 3) The other person(s) needs to be forgiven

Appendix D

Self-Control

Week 1: OOCE #1: Delayed Gratification   Name_____

Choose a simple daily task or chore, such as walking the dog or doing the dishes. Be sure to choose simple tasks rather than ones that are substantial or special. Decide on some type of healthy or enjoyable thing you want. Examples could include a favorite food, a moderate amount of chocolate or reading some of your favorite book. Delay permitting yourself from having that thing until you have completed your chosen task. Do this a total of three times in a week. This task is further refined in the next session.

Record the experience of delaying the gratification, answering the questions in the table below:

1) What was the daily task you completed?
2) What was the reward used?

Rate the following two questions based on the following scale:
1 = not at all; 2 = not really; 3 = undecided; 4 = somewhat; 5 = very

Q1) Was the delay of gratification difficult?
Q2) Did you feel you enjoyed the delayed reward more?

	1) Daily Task	2) Reward	Q1	Q2
Day 1	_____	_____	_____	_____
Day 2	_____	_____	_____	_____
Day 3	_____	_____	_____	_____

Week 2: OOCE #2:   Name_____

Reverse the exercise from the previous session. For example, you want a cold soda. Delay getting the soda until you have completed a pre-determined task that is SELF-ASSIGNED.

This task should not be routine. Maybe you will call a significant other or parent and ask how their day is going. Do this a total of three times in a week.

Record the experience of delaying the gratification, answering the questions in the table below:

1) What was the task you completed?
2) What was the reward used?

Rate the following two questions based on the following scale:
1 = not at all; 2 = not really; 3 = undecided; 4 = somewhat; 5 = very

Q1) Was the delay of gratification difficult?
Q2) Did you feel you enjoyed the delayed reward more?

(1) Task	(2) Reward	Q1	Q2
Day 1_____	_____	_____	_____
Day 2_____	_____	_____	_____
Day 3_____	_____	_____	_____

Week 3: ICE Scenario 1, part 1:   Name_____

You are at work. You are assigned to write a report with a co-worker. The report is due in two days. You are dependent on the co-worker completing their part of the report before you can complete your portion. The report cannot be late, and it must be accurate. When you go to look for the co-worker, you find them in the break room, with a cup of coffee, talking to another co-worker. You ask for the report and they respond that they are not done. At this point you explode. You start yelling at the co-worker. They are surprised by your verbal attack and they yell back. On the table in front of your co-worker you see some papers and knock them on the floor. You storm out of the break room.

A. Which STS did you apply?:
Communicating Calmly:_____ Time-out:_____ Active Listening:_____
Perspective Thinking:_____ Win/Win to No Deal: _____

B. Consider your next step.

Rate each of the following possibilities based on the scale below:

1 = very easy; 2 = somewhat easy; 3 = undecided; 4 = somewhat difficulty; 5 = very difficult;

B1. Go back and apologize for your outburst: _____

B2. Calm down: _____

B3. Listen to the co-worker's issues: _____

B4. Focus on the solution instead of the deadline: _____

C. Which action do you believe you should take? Select only one.

C1. Report the actions of your co-worker to your supervisor: _____

C2. Apologize to your co-worker for your outburst. Then go to your supervisor: _____

C3. Sit down with your co-worker and determine what is causing the delay: _____

C4. Both of you go see the supervisor to discuss the project: _____

Week 3: ICE Scenario 1, part 2: Name_____

You come back from a quick walk around the building and find your co-worker in their office, working on the report. You calmly ask why it is taking them so long to complete their part of the report. They respond that some of the information for the report is changing. This will affect the outcome of the report. The person to whom they were speaking in the break-room was explaining the changes. You start becoming angry because instead of coming to you, they left you "hanging" rather than discussing the issues. By not speaking to you they have jeopardized your job and the time-table of the assignment.

How difficult would it be to use the following STS's?

Use the following rating system:

1 = very easy; 2 = somewhat easy; 3 = undecided; 4 = somewhat difficult; 5 = very difficult

A. Remain Calm _____

B. Listen and then have them listen to you _____

C. Keep the situation in perspective _____

D. Step out of the office to remain calm _____

E. Empathize with the co-worker _____

F. Figure out if your job is really at risk _____

The following exercise requires you to record your anger episodes. Part of this course develops long-term strategies (LTS) for the treatment of a variety of anger styles. In regard to short-term strategies (STS), anger may be viewed as either more outward or more inward.

Outward anger is typical of the Explosive Anger Styles. By initially learning to walk away, a person develops and demonstrates self-control. Strategies, such as communicating calmly or active listening, also involve elements of self-control.

Inward anger is a little more difficult to self-assess. The typical example is the passive aggressive person who rarely directly confronts people with whom they are angry. If you tend to use this anger style, you must determine when you are feeling anger. You must then notice your desire to respond in your usual way. Instead of walking off angry, procrastinating, sabotaging a project, or making snippy comments, you should use one of the short-term strategies that involve dealing with the problem. For example, someone assigns you a short project that you must complete. Honestly and tactfully explain you are not able to put forth your best effort at this time (communicating calmly). Perhaps ask for more time or get clarification on the importance of the task. All of this requires the use of self-control.

Measurement for Self-Control: Self-Evaluation:

After each anger episode, list the following items in the table below:

- A short description of the episode
- Did the episode occur in the AM or PM?
- The STS used. A partial list follows after the chart.
- The difficulty you had using the strategy.

Rate the difficulty using the following scale:
1 = very easy; 2 = somewhat easy; 3 = undecided; 4 = somewhat difficult; 5 = very difficult

Difficulty #	Anger Episode Description	AM/PM	STS Used	Difficulty Using Strategy
Day 1: 1_____	_____	_____	_____	_____
2_____	_____	_____	_____	_____

Day 2: 1_____ _____ _____ _____ _____
       2_____ _____ _____ _____ _____

Day 3: 1_____ _____ _____ _____ _____
       2_____ _____ _____ _____ _____

You may use any STS that is effective for you. Be sure to record any strategy used. Below are some (but not all) of the possible STS's.

Abdominal Breathing: Slowly inhale and exhale, expanding the diaphragm.

Time-out: If losing control, calmly/politely leave, de-stress, then return and solve the problem.

Win/Win to No Deal: Communicate clearly and politely, working toward a solution.

Active Listening: Listen to the other parties with the intention they will also listen to you.

Communicating Calmly: Communicate so as to encourage others to communicate in the same way.

Week 1:

In the first week we work on a very basic level of self-control. Participants choose a daily task and a reward at the completion of that task. This adds a level "one" of self-control.

Week 2:

A level of complexity is added to the assignment from week 1. The exercise involves applying self-control, at will, on a simple task. Instead of a daily or routine task, the reward is contingent on completing a self-assigned task. They deny themselves the reward until the task has been completed. An example could be wanting a chocolate bar. The assigned task might be calling a parent or loved one with whom they have not spoken in a while. They would have no chocolate until the call was completed.

Week 3: OOCE 3:

Most anger escalates because one or both of the individuals either lose control, or fail to stop a negative pattern (cognitive or behavioral) from continuing. The exercises were simple, achievable demonstrations that increased in difficulty of self-control. The concept of confirming to the individual that they have the ability to successfully apply self-control, raises their self-control confidence. Even in the middle of an anger episode, that will translate into greater confidence to allow them to successfully maintain self-control.

The passive-aggressive (PA) individual will automatically default to focusing their lack of cooperation by projecting it at the person with whom they are angry. As a long-term strategy, when a situation occurs where the PA is projecting, they should instead honestly state that, "I have not fully embraced the task and may not have given it my best effort." This is difficult to do at the onset. It is easier by starting with statements such as, "Let me work on the project/task a bit more." In this statement, the PA is not making any direct admissions, but has interrupted the usual cycle of projection onto the PA's target individual. This step is resisting the PA pattern and involves exhibiting self-control.

For explosive anger styles, the initial demonstration of self-control might be simply walking away from the situation/event at the onset. By exercising this level of self-control, the individual can expand levels of self-control. For both types of anger styles, the participants should record the number of anger episodes and the number of times they were able to exert self-control over themselves and interrupt the behavior cycle.

The counselor/group leader should count the number of STS's being deployed, as well as the spectrum of strategies.

- How many anger episodes do they have per week?
- Does the participant primarily rely on one or two strategies?
- Are they able to apply strategies in broad and diverse ways?
- Is there a pattern to the anger episodes? Are they every day, every other day, at night, etc?

Look to see if the participants are versatile in their strategy use. A participant that only used the time-out strategy might be reinforcing a pattern of anger avoidance.

Results and Scoring:

There are 5 exercises for skill training and gauging the effectiveness of skill development. The skill training is a combination of self-delayed gratification (exercises 1 and 2; out of class; and application of self-control in anger situations (3.1 - 3.3). In all of these exercises, the level of difficulty increases. The first exercise focuses on a daily or routine task identified by the participant, along with a reward they will permit themselves once the routine task is completed. Because the task is done daily, and generally people do not reward themselves for the completion of routine tasks, the enjoyment of the reward should score (mean) higher than the difficulty in delaying the gratification (mean).

In the second exercise, the task is not routine and self-assigned. Under these conditions it is anticipated that the enjoyment of the reward would be greater. If this is the case, generally speaking, the degree of difficulty should either increase (mean) or decrease for the first exercise. If the degree of delay was more difficult, it would indicate that the individual had to apply more energy and diligence to the delay, which indicates the need to improve the skill. A decrease, or equal, in the delay score (mean) from the first exercise delay score, indicates the individual has a higher level of self-control.

As the exercises continue from 3.1 to 3.3, they get progressively more difficult. If the score for applying a non-confrontational STS to an anger episode decreases, it indicates the person requires more skill training and that the skill training is not effecting measureable change. If the individual's mean delay score increases, it indicates the participant was able to apply the skills of Self-control to a real-world anger situation. A decrease between 3.1 and 3.2 indicates the degree of difficulty between the exercises. An increase in 3.3 mean delay score indicates that in a real-life situation, the individual was able to effectively apply skills of self-control to the implementation of STS during anger episode

Scoring:

In total, there are 5 exercises for this self-control instrument. The scoring involves normalizing all of the answers in order to generate a number between 1 and 3. The exercise difficulty increases from week 1 to week 3. So, a 2.0 scored in week 1 shows less self-control than a 2.0 scored in week 3. This is how progress (or deterioration) in the skill (over the course of the 3 weeks) is shown. Plot the final score for each exercise into the comparative graph for the 5 exercises. Plot the actual numbers so that the differences can be seen from week to week. The scores are also grouped according to the following scale:

A score of 1.0 to 1.9 is low Self-control.
A score greater than 1.9 up to 2.9 is moderate self-control.
A score of greater than 2.9 and less than or equal to 3 is high self-control.

Week 1: OOCE #1:

If question 1 is rated as a 1, that shows high self-control and is scored as 3 points.
If question 1 is rated as a 2 or a 3, that is moderate self-control and is scored as 2 points.
If question 1 is rated as a 4 or a 5, that is low self-control and is scored as 1 point.
Average the scores of the 3 self-assigned tasks. This generates a score between 1.0 and 3.0 for week 1 OOCE.

Week 2: OOCE #2:

Use the same scoring as in week 1.

Week 3: ICE Scenario 1, part 1:

This exercise has 3 parts: A, B, and C. Determine the score for each of these parts as follows:

A: If they marked "Win/Win to No Deal" and/or "Time-out", this is assigned 3 points.
If they marked any other answer, in any combination, they are to only get 1 point for part A.
This generates a score of either 1 or 3 for part A.

B: Convert their answers using the following scale:
1 = 3 points; 2 or 3 = 2 points; 4 or a 5 = 1 point
Add all of their points together and divide by 4. This generates a number between 1.0 and 3.0 for part B.

C: They may only select one answer for this part.
Answer C1 = 1 point; Answers C2 or C4 = 2 points; Answer C3 = 3 points
This generates a score of either 1, 2, or 3 for part C.

Take the score for part A and multiply it by .25 _____

Take the average score for part B and multiply it by .5 _____
Take the score for part C and multiply it by .25 _____

The difficulty assigned in implementing the various strategies (part B), has more weight than parts A and C.
Add the three scores for A,B, and C together.   (total) _____
This generates a score between 1.0 and 3.0 for the week 3 ICE Scenario 1, part 1.

Week 3: ICE Scenario 1, part 2:

Questions A through F are scored in the following fashion:
1 = 3 points; 2 or 3 = 2 points; 4 or a 5 = 1 point
Add up the points. Divide by 5. This generates a score between 1.0 and 3.0 for Week 3 ICE Scenario 1, part 2.

Week 3: OOCE #3:
The participants should have given three examples of when they used a short-term strategy regarding anger. To some degree, this is a reflection of self-control. They were to record any three incidences during that week. For some, they may not have had three incidences where they were very angry. Regardless, even a low-anger situation qualifies for the exercise of some self-control.

The scoring for this exercise is as follows:
1 = 3 points; 2 or 3 = 2 points; 4 or a 5 = 1 point

Add up the points and divide by the number of anger episodes they recorded. This generates a number between 1.0 and 3.0 for this exercise.

Appendix E

Empathy

Week 1: ICE Scenario 1, part 1A: Name_____

Read the following scenario and answer the proceeding questions.

You are driving to the store, listening to music. As you enter the parking lot of the store, another car enters at the same time, heading straight for you. You swerve, narrowly missing their car. You look up and notice the driver staring ahead intently and frowning. You find a parking spot and head into the store. After searching for what you want, you hear another person raising their voice with a salesperson. You walk around the aisle and see them both at the far end. The salesperson says something you cannot hear. The person puts their left hand on their forehead and shakes their head slightly. You recognize them as the driver of the vehicle you almost crashed into. The person loudly says, "You are useless" and rapidly walks out of your line of sight.

1a. What are the emotions you believe the person is exhibiting/feeling?

Aggravation_____   Anger_____   Anxiety_____   Fear_____

Frustration_____   Irritation_____   Love_____   Sadness_____

Happiness_____   Other_____

2a. What are the cues they are experiencing these feelings?

_____   _____

_____   _____

_____   _____

3a. Does it appear these feelings were caused by something before or after they arrived?

Before:_____   After:_____   Possibly Both:_____

4a. How confident are you that the emotions selected were correct? _____

1 = not at all confident; 2 = somewhat confident; 3 = very confident

5a. How difficult was it to determine the cues? _____
1 = not at all difficult; 2 = somewhat difficult; 3 = very difficult

6a. Have you experienced a situation like this before, yes or no? _____

7a. Have you ever felt the same way as this person? (rate 1 to 3) _____
1 = never; 2 = somewhat; 3 = exactly

8a. How easy was it for you to recall an example of when you felt the same way? _____
1 = not at all easy; 2 = somewhat easy; 3 = very easy

Week 1: ICE Scenario 1, part 2B: Name_____

As you near the cash register check-out, you notice the same person in the check-out line with their back toward you. The person is tapping their feet and occasionally glancing at the screen on their phone. The phone rings while they are paying for their items, and the person answers. You see the person take a deep breath; then smile, nod their head, and say something you cannot hear. The person continues their conversation, smiling and talking as they walk toward the door and exit the store.

1b. What are the emotions you believe the customer is exhibiting/feeling?
Aggravation_____ Anger_____ Anxiety_____ Fear_____
Frustration_____ Irritation_____ Love_____ Sadness_____
Happiness_____ Other_____

2b. What are the cues they are experiencing these feelings?
_____   _____
_____   _____

3b. Does it appear these feelings were caused by something before or after they arrived?
Before_____ After_____ Possibly Both_____

4b. How confident are you that the emotions selected were correct? _____
1 = not at all confident; 2 = somewhat confident; 3 = very confident

5b How difficult was it to determine the cues? _____
1 = not at all difficult; 2 = somewhat difficult; 3 = very difficult

6b. Have you experienced a situation like this before, yes or no? _____

7b. Have you ever felt the same way as this person? (rate 1 to 3) _____

8b. How easy was it to recall an example of when you felt the same way? _____
1 = not at all easy; 2 = somewhat easy; 3 = very easy

Week 1: OOCE #A: Name_____

Follow these instructions and answer the proceeding questions.

- Go to a public place, such as a restaurant, workplace, subway, or coffee shop. Observe the physical and emotional gestures and cues of others. This may include facial expressions, posture, tone of voice, and other signs.
- Politely and discreetly observe someone from a non-intrusive distance.

1a. What are the emotions you believe the person is exhibiting/feeling?
Aggravation_____   Anger_____   Anxiety_____   Fear_____
Frustration_____   Irritation_____   Love_____   Sadness_____
Happiness_____   Other_____

2a. What are the cues they are experiencing these feelings?
_____   _____
_____   _____

3a. Does it appear these feelings were caused by something before or after they arrived?
Before_____   After_____   Possibly Both_____

4a. How confident are you that the emotions selected are correct? _____
1 = not at all confident; 2 = somewhat confident; 3 = very confident

5a. How difficult was it to determine the cues? _____
1 = not at all difficult; 2 = somewhat difficult; 3 = very difficult

- Find someone who will honestly discuss their feelings with you; preferably a close friend or relative.
- Ask them the following questions, giving them enough time to answer. Record their answer below.
- Say to them, "I am taking a class involving emotions and need your help for an assignment. I would like to take a few minutes to ask you three questions about an emotional experience you have had. Are you ok with that?" If yes, proceed to ask them questions 1b-3b. Afterward, you answer questions 4b-6b.

1b. Please tell me about a time when you felt irritated or angry (pissed off) and people did not understand what you were feeling.

_____

_____

2b. What did they do that made you feel or think you were not understood?

_____

_____

3b. What could they have done to make the situation better?

_____

_____

4b. Have you experienced a situation like this before, yes or no? _____

5b. Have you ever felt the same way as this person (rate 1 to 3) _____
1 = never; 2 = somewhat; 3 = exactly

6b. How easy was it for you to recall an example of when you felt the same way? _____
1 = not at all easy; 2 = somewhat easy; 3 = very easy

Week 2: ICE Scenario 2, part 1A: Name_____

Read the following scenario and answer the proceeding questions.

You are a member of a church community. After attending a service you are outside the church talking with some friends and family. You notice across the parking lot a friend of yours in an intense discussion with their spouse. The spouse is jabbing their finger at your friend and then points at their own chest. Without looking up the spouse points in your general direction. Your friend looks up and begins moving toward you. Their lips are tightly pursed and they are shaking their head slightly. When they approach, they begin arguing with you and say, "You are a loser. Stay away from me and my family". You are not sure what they are talking about. You ask, "What the hell is this about?" Looking downward, with their hands on their hips, they take a forced breath. They go on to curse at you, calling you names. Your friend is yelling about their spouse and your behavior. The name calling has begun making you angry. Your friend then pokes you hard in the chest with their finger, turns away, and storms off.

1a. What are the emotions you believe your friend is exhibiting/feeling?
Aggravation_____ Anger_____ Anxiety_____ Fear_____
Frustration_____ Irritation_____ Love_____ Sadness_____
Happiness_____ Other_____

2a. What are the cues they are experiencing these feelings?
_____   _____
_____   _____

3a. Does it appear these feelings were caused by something before or after they arrived?
Before_____ After_____ Possibly Both_____

4a. How confident are you that the emotions selected were correct? _____
1 = not at all confident; 2 = somewhat confident; 3 = very confident

5a. How difficult was it to determine the cues? _____
1 = not at all difficult; 2 = somewhat difficult; 3 = very difficult

6a. Have you experienced a situation like your friend's, yes or no? _____

7a. Have you ever felt the same way as your friend? (rate 1 to 3) _____
1 = never; 2 = somewhat; 3 = exactly

8a. How easy was it for you to recall an example of when you felt the same way? _____
1 = not at all easy; 2 = somewhat easy; 3 = very easy

Week 2: ICE Scenario 2, part 2B: Name_____

Other church members begin commenting on what they saw. Some seem to be taking the side of your friend. Your friend's father is a church leader. The outburst carries the risk of you no longer being welcomed in the church. You walk after your friend, catching up with then near their car. Your friend scowls when they see it is you and then looks off as if they do not see you. You have your hands extended, palms facing your friend. You say, "Look, I do not want to argue or fight. If I just listen, would you be willing to explain exactly what this is about?" You are thinking of just walking off, but your patience is rewarded with an answer.

Your friend states that you were staring at their spouse. You say, "This may be a misunderstanding. If I looked at your spouse, I did not even notice." Your friend stands with their hands on their hips, looking down and listening.

1b. What are the emotions you believe your friend is exhibiting/feeling?
Aggravation_____   Anger_____   Anxiety_____   Fear_____
Frustration_____   Irritation_____   Love_____   Sadness_____
Happiness_____   Other_____

2b. What are the cues your friend is experiencing these feelings?
_____   _____   _____
_____   _____   _____

3b. Does it appear these feelings were caused by something before or after they arrived?
Before_____ After_____ Possibly Both_____

4b. How confident are you that the emotions selected were correct? _____
1 = not at all confident; 2 = somewhat confident; 3 = very confident

5b. How difficult was it to determine the cues? _____
1 = not at all difficult; 2 = somewhat difficult; 3 = very difficult

6b. Have you experienced a situation like your friend's, yes or no? _____

7b. Have you ever felt the same way as your friend? (rate 1 to 3) _____
1 = never; 2 = somewhat; 3 = exactly

8b. How easy was it for you to recall an example of when you felt the same way? _____
1 = not at all easy; 2 = somewhat easy; 3 = very easy

Week 2: OOCE A & B:

Repeat the week 1 OOCE's A & B. Follow the same instructions, answering the accompanying questions.

Week 1/scenario 1, part 1A:

The scenarios are designed to provide clear physical emotional cues. The emotions associated with the cues are ambiguous out of design. Questions 1-5 relate to the identification of physical cues. Questions 6-8 involve participants identifying emotions in the scenario and relating them to emotions they have experienced. Here are some things to consider when assessing the answers of the participants:

- Accounting for some ambiguity, are the cues and emotions accurately identified by the participant?
- Is there consistency between the observed cues and the observed emotions?
- If the emotions and cues are correctly identified, are they easily able to relate it to their own experiences? (Questions 4-8)
- Are they identifying more than one emotion or multiple emotions?

Week 1/scenario 1, part 2B:

A small level of complexity is added to the scenarios with participants answering the same sets of questions. The individual in the scenario obviously goes through an emotional change. The added information of the cell phone call should put the scenario into the perspective that the feelings (of the various agitated states) were either caused by something before or possibly BOTH before and after (question 3b).

One would expect some correlations between some of the questions. For instance, perceptive yet low-empathy individuals might correctly identify the emotional states (question 1) and the cues (question 2). Yet, they might be moderately confident or "not at all confident".

Scenario 1, part 1A

1a. The most likely expressed emotions in scenario 1, in no particular order, are 6 emotions: Aggravation, Irritation, Anger, Sadness, Anxiety, and Frustration.

Scoring:
4 or more correctly identified emotions =3; 3 emotions = 2; 2 or less = 1
If they mark or identify an incorrect emotion, subtract one from their score. If they mark or identify 2 or more incorrect emotions, score them as a 1. Any score below a 1 is still recorded as a "1", which is the lowest possible score.

2a. The spectrum of possible emotions was kept broad based on the broad range of cues. There are 7 overt physical/emotional cues in the scenario:
1) staring ahead intently 2) frowning 3) raised voice 4) left hand on forehead 5) shakes head slightly 6) disparaging comment (you are useless) 7) rapidly walks off

Scoring:
Correctly identifying 5 or more cues = 3; 3-4 cues = 2; 2 or less cues = 1.

4a. and 5a.
Simply record their answers for these questions (1, 2, or 3).

Scenario 1, part 2B:
1b. The possible emotions are:
Happiness, Anxiety, Aggravation, Irritation, Frustration, or Other (Any moderate emotions relating to calmness/relief).

Scoring:
4 or more correctly identified emotions = 3; 3 emotions = 2; 2 or less = 1.
If they marked or identified an incorrect emotion, subtract one from their score. If they mark or identify 2 or more incorrect emotions, score them as a 1. Any score below a 1 is still recorded as a "1", which is the lowest possible score.

2b. The number of cues is 5:
1) tapping foot 2) nodding their head 3) staring repeatedly at their phone screen
4) conversation and smiling 5) deep breath and smile

Scoring:
Correctly identifying 4 or more cues = 3; 3 cues = 2; 2 or less cues = 1.

4b. and 5b.
Simply record their answers for these questions.

Scenario 2, part 1A:
1a. The possible emotions are:
Aggravation, Irritation, Anger, Frustration, Anxiety, and Other (Jealousy).

Scoring:
4 or more correctly identified emotions = 3; 3 emotions = 2; 2 or less = 1.
If they mark or identify an incorrect emotion, subtract one from their score. If they mark or identify 2 or more incorrect emotions, score them as a 1. Any score below a 1 is still recorded as a "1", which is the lowest possible score.

2a. There are 10 cues:
1) intense discussion 2) spouse jabbing finger, then points at own chest 3) lips tightly pursed 4) shaking head 5) arguing 6) disparaging comments / attacking 7) name calling 8) looking down, hands on hips, deep breath 9) anger 10) pokes finger in chest
Scoring:
Correctly identifying 6 or more cues = 3; 5-3 cues = 2; 2 or less cues = 1.

4a. and 5a.
Simply record their answers to these questions (1, 2, or 3).

Scenario 2, part 2B:
1b. The possible emotions are:
Aggravation, Anxiety, Anger, Frustration, Irritation, Other (Jealousy), or Other (Any moderate emotions relating to calmness or relief).

Scoring:
4 or more correctly identified emotions = 3; 3 emotions = 2; 2 or less = 1.
If they mark or identify an incorrect emotion, subtract one from their score. If they mark or identify 2 or more incorrect emotions, score them as a 1. Any score below a 1 is still recorded as a "1", which is the lowest possible score.

2b. There are 7 cues:
1) scowls 2) ignores (not seeing you) 3) not wanting to fight 4) willing to listen 5) hands extended, palms out 6) showing patience 7) listening

Scoring:
Correctly identifying 5 or more cues = 3; 3-4 cues = 2; 2 or less cues = 1.

4b. and 5b.
Simply record their answers to these questions (1, 2, or 3).

Appendix F

Forgiveness of Others

Week 1: ICE Scenario 1, part 1:   Name_____

You and a co-worker are both being considered for promotion for the same position. The promotion comes with a substantial increase in pay and responsibility. You have both been asked to submit a report, which you do. Your competitor points out to your mutual supervisor that your report was based on outdated information. The part of your report that had outdated information was actually supplied by your competitor. Because of your poor report, your supervisor ends up promoting your competitor instead of you. You find out that your competitor placed the newer and correct information into their report. As a result of failing to get the promotion, you cannot afford to place your aging and ailing mother into an adult living facility. Prior to this, your relationship with your competitor was polite and pleasant. You barge into their office the next day. You yell at them for giving you the outdated information. An argument erupts, but is interrupted when the supervisor's office asks to see your competitor about something else. You leave the office angry, resentful, and frustrated. However, you still have to continue to work with this person every day.

Exercise A
Rate the following questions using this scale:
1 = not at all; 2 = not really; 3 = undecided; 4 = probably yes; 5 = absolutely

When you next confront this person(s) you intend to:
1a) Ignore the person for fear for losing your temper   _____
2a) Have a calm and professional discussion   _____
3a) Offer forgiveness to the person(s)   _____

Exercise B
Rate the following questions using this scale:
1 = not at all; 2 = not really; 3 = undecided; 4 = probably yes; 5 = absolutely

In the future, regarding this person(s), you will:

1b) Hold a grudge or resent the other person _____

2b) Wish physical or emotional harm to the other person(s) _____

3b) Become angry whenever you talk or think about the situation _____

Week 1: ICE Scenario 2, part 1 (hypothetical example): Name_____

You come home from work and find your spouse and child have been murdered. Over the course of the next two weeks the murderer is identified and arrested.

Exercise C

Rate the following questions using this scale:

1 = not at all; 2 = not really; 3 = undecided; 4 = probably yes; 5 = absolutely

Regarding this situation I feel:

1c) I am willing to sit down and listen to their explanation of why they murdered my family. _____

2c) The law's punishment will be sufficient for me to begin my emotional healing process. _____

3c) I am willing to consider forgiving them. _____

Exercise D

Rate the following questions using this scale:

1 = not at all; 2 = not really; 3 = undecided; 4 = probably yes; 5 = absolutely

In regards to this person:

1d) I wish any physical or emotional harm upon them. _____

2d) I hate the murderer, even if they are put to death and even if the hate is unhealthy for me. _____

3d) Whenever I talk or think about the situation, it makes me angry. _____

Week 1: OOCE #1 (3 parts):   Name_____

Answer the following 6 questions in regards to any real-life situation you have experienced or are currently experiencing. Do not use extreme scenarios, such as the hypothetical example of the murder of one's family.

Part I - Describe the situation in the space below:

_____

_____

_____

Part II - Rate the following questions using this scale:
1 = not at all; 2 = not really; 3 = undecided; 4 = somewhat interested; 5 = very interested

When you next confront this person(s) you intend to:
1a) Listen to their explanation of their actions. _____
2a) Have a calm and professional discussion. _____
3a) Offer forgiveness to the person(s). _____

Part III - Rate the following questions using this scale:
1 = not at all; 2 = not really; 3 = undecided; 4 = somewhat; 5 = absolutely

In the future, regarding this person(s), you will:
1b) Hold a grudge or resent the person. _____
2b) Wish physical or emotional harm to the other person(s). _____
3b) Become angry whenever you talk to think about the situation. _____

Week 2: ICE Scenario 1, part 2 (Resolution to Scenario 1): Name_____

Both you and your competitor use the same bank. A friend of your competitor works at the bank. They inform you that you competitor's spouse is fighting cancer. The family has been struggling financially for over a year with substantial costs not covered under their health plan. The person sharing this information has done this without knowing about the report and promotion issue.

Exercise E
Rate the following questions using this scale:
1 = not at all; 2 = not really; 3 = undecided; 4 = probably yes; 5 = absolutely

1e) This new information modifies my opinion of the person. _____
2e) I should have a professional discussion to resolve this issue. _____
3e) If they are willing to apologize for the harm caused, I would forgive them. _____

4e) Even if they will not apologize for the harm caused, I am willing to forgive them for my sake, not theirs. _____

Exercise F

Rate the following questions using this scale:

1 = not at all; 2 = not really; 3 = undecided; 4 = probably yes; 5 = absolutely

1f) What my competitor did was wrong and I will hold a grudge or resent them. _____

2f) I wish them harm physically or emotionally. _____

3f) In the future, it will make me angry whenever I talk or think about the situation. _____

Week 2: ICE Scenario 2, part 2 (Additional Information) Name_____

After a lengthy trial, the murderer was found guilty and will be sentenced to death by lethal injection. While they are on death row, a medical examination is performed on them. It is discovered that the murderer has a chemical imbalance in their brain that creates uncontrollable psychotic rage.

Exercise G

Rate the following questions using this scale:

1 = not at all; 2 = not really; 3 = undecided; 4 = probably yes; 5 = absolutely

1g) I am willing to sit down and listen to their explanation. _____

2g) The law's punishment will be sufficient for me to begin my emotional healing process. _____

3g) I am willing to consider forgiving their actions. _____

Exercise H

Rate the following questions using this scale:

1 = not at all; 2 = not really; 3 = undecided; 4 = probably yes; 5 = absolutely

1h) I wish them any type of pain or harm. _____

2h) I hate the murderer, even if they are put to death and the hate is unhealthy for me. _____

3h) In the future, it will make me angry whenever I talk or think about the situation. _____

Consider a current or recent issue you have where someone has harmed you and the situation is not resolved and forgiven. Have a calm discussion with the other person about the situation. Consider forgiveness as a way to finally resolve the situation. Use the active listening skills that have been developed in the course. If there is a chance of the situation escalating into violence, or if you hate rather than resent them, do not approach the person for a discussion.

Answer question 1 below. After completing out-of-class exercise 2, answer the remaining questions.

Part I - Record below an unresolved situation that you currently have.

_____

_____

_____

Part II - Rate the following questions using this scale:
1 = not at all; 2 = not really; 3 = undecided; 4 = somewhat interested; 5 = very interested

When you next confront this person(s) you intend to:
1a) Listen to their explanation for their actions.   _____
2a) Have a calm and professional discussion.   _____
3a) Offer forgiveness to the person(s)   _____

Part III - Rate the following questions using this scale:
1 = not at all; 2 = not really; 3 = undecided; 4 = somewhat; 5 = absolutely

In the future, regarding this person(s) you will:
1b) Hold a grudge or resent the person.   _____
2b) Wish physical or emotional harm to the other person(s).   _____
3b) Become angry whenever you talk or think about the situation.   _____

Part IV
1) Did you have a discussion with this person(s)? (circle one) Y / N

2) If no, why not?

_____

_____

Week 3: OOCE #3: Final Exercise: Name_____.

Rate the following questions using this scale:
1 = not at all; 2 = not really; 3 = undecided; 4 = somewhat; 5 = absolutely

1) I find it easier to forgive friends and family than co-workers. _____

2) I find it easier to forgive co-workers than friends and family. _____

3) When I forgive someone, it is to benefit me. _____

4) When I forgive someone, it is to benefit both of us. _____

5) I could forgive the co-worker in scenario 1 (see below). _____

6) In scenario 2 (see below), I could let go of my hate, because the justice system gave me a way to release it. _____

Scenario 1 (review):

You and a co-worker are both being considered for promotion for the same position. The promotion comes with a substantial increase in pay and responsibility. You both have been asked to submit a report. Your competitor points out to your mutual supervisor that your report was based on outdated information. The part of your report that had outdated information was actually supplied by your competitor. Because of your poor report, your supervisor ends up promoting your competitor instead of you. You find out that your competitor placed the newer and correct information into their report. As a result of missing the promotion, you cannot afford to place your aging and ailing mother into an adult living facility. Prior to this, your relationship with your competitor was polite and pleasant. You barge into their office the next day. You yell at them for giving you the outdated information. An argument erupts, but is interrupted when the supervisor's office asks to see your competitor about something else. You leave the office angry, resentful, and frustrated. However, you still have to continue to work with this person every day.

Both you and your competitor use the same bank. A friend of your competitor works at the bank. They inform you that your competitor's spouse is fighting cancer. The family has been struggling financially for over a year with substantial costs not covered under their health plan. The person sharing this information has done this without knowing about the report and promotion issue.

Scenario 2 / hypothetical example (review):

You come home from work and find your spouse and child have been murdered. Over the course of the next two weeks the murderer is identified and arrested. After a lengthy trail, the murderer was found guilty and will be sentenced to death by lethal injection. While they are on death row, a medical examination is performed on them. It is discovered that the murderer has a chemical imbalance in their brain that creates uncontrollable psychotic rage.

Skill Building Analysis:
The exercises are designed as a two-step approach to develop cognitive skill building toward forgiveness of others. The primary goals of this approach are to assist participants to recognize that forgiveness should be seen as a resolution, and can benefit both individuals, but certainly benefits the person conveying forgiveness.

Forgiveness: Week 1: Analysis of Exercises:
The first week involves two hypothetical scenarios. Through these scenarios we are developing 3 foundational skills, and participants should learn the following:

1. Non-harmful resolution is the first focus. The benefits to oneself for forgiving others are taught by the second set of questions.
2. The potential steps to resolve a situation vs. the destructive planning of resentment.
3. Severe situations, such as the murder scenario, do not have the same burden of resolution. Such situations can be delegated to an appropriate outside force (focus of control).

No interaction is necessary in order to apply the first six questions to a real-life situation. The first step is for the individual to incorporate a resolution mind-set to a negative situation (the first three questions). They are then asked to reevaluate the situation. There is an underlying reason for the separation of the first set from the second set of questions, with a repeat of the rating scale. The second set of questions are written to illustrate to the person harmed, the possible negative, long-term ramifications of not forgiving.

Forgiveness: Week 2: Expansion of Skills:

The addition of information is to walk the participant through a progressive evaluation process. In scenario 1, the additional information of the competitor's wife's health is added. It is not added as an excuse, but a possible reason for the competitor's actions. There is no instruction provided as to whether the negative behavior is unusual for the competitor, or if it is their behavioral norm. The information is intended to:

1. Elicit empathy.
2. Develop optimism by suggesting that a resolution may be possible.
3. Suggest that the competitor's actions might be forgivable.

The questions are slightly altered to suggest the unhealthy consequences for the person harmed.

Scenario 2 helps with the following skills:

1. The murderer has a neurological disorder which may have influenced their behavior. This may elicit some empathy despite the terrible outcome.
2. One should relinquish part of the closure to the judicial process. This suggests transferring part of the resolution to an outside entity.
3. The only person hurt by hatred is the victim. The questions are focused on the issue of resolution and the importance of extinguishing this hate. Thesis not necessarily done through Forgiveness, but is accomplished by abandoning hate.

Scenario 1 hopefully represents a more likely scenario than the murder scenario. The counselor should look at the gradient of change between the week 1 and week 2 exercises. If the participants are learning and applying the intended skills, two measurable changes should be observed.

1. The participants should rate the first week's questions with a more visceral reaction, rating resolution as a lower desire. After the introduction of the week 2 additional scenario information, they should see a gradient change toward increase in resolution oriented actions. Individuals with potentially more skill with self-forgiveness may rate resolution tendencies higher, or possibly neutral in week one.
2. In scenario 2, the severe aberrant harm is intended to elicit as strong an emotional response as possible. This scenario is not intended to promote forgiveness. Most

individuals with a reasonably healthy psyche would not be able to forgive the murderer. We are focused on the skills recognizing that any form of hate, no matter how justified, is destructive to the hater. By delegating the constructive justice (the victim NOT killing the murderer) and accepting the justice system, or any outside social construct to take over the role of resolution, and if the individual can attach their emotion of hate to the decision, then the destructive components of hate can be released as a burden of the victim. This leaves them addressing the emotions related to traumatic loss.

There may be correlations between an individual's anger style and the gradient of responses within each week and between each week's exercises. As an example, passive-aggressive (PA) individuals who are struggling with self-forgiveness, may rate lower on the gradient. Individuals with excitatory anger may see the scenarios as an opportunity to accelerate their anger. In that case, the gradient rating might move in the other direction. The gradient could also remain neutral, because participants do not want to appear uncooperative or not improving to the counselor. The participant knows what the expected responses are, but may not be able to rate themselves into the resolution gradient.

OOCE #2:
Confirm with the participants that while practicing these skills in real life situations is ideal, they do not (should not) do so in any situation which may deteriorate into any form of physical conflict or altercation.

Additional analysis including seeking correlations may become apparent as the data is collected. Because this, like the other Virtue/Strength/Skill (VSS) exercises are the first mechanism of applying positive psychology, all results cannot be anticipated. For ongoing VSS forgiveness development, continue the week 2 OOCE #2.

The following is further suggested reading, dealing with forgiveness and related subjects:

* *A Course in Miracles*, Dr. Helen Shuman and Dr. William Thetford, Foundation for Inner Peace, Huntington Station: NY (1975) This work combines the practice of forgiveness with a unique perspective on the Bible.

* *Authentic Happiness*, Martin E.P. Seligman, PhD, Simon & Schuster: NY (2002)

* *The Power of Now*, Eckhart Tolle, Namaste Publishing, Vancouver: BC, (1999)

This book is primarily concerned with focusing one's awareness on the present moment. Actively applied, this book can free one from negative thinking related to the past or from anxiety from projecting into the future.

* Take the Forgiveness Quiz. http://greatergood/berkley.edu/quizzes/take_quiz2
This site has useful information on Forgiveness and other positive psychology topics. The quiz is informative on how likely you are to forgive at this time. Based upon your score, it has suggestions on what you can do now to forgive.

Forgiveness Scoring, interpretation, and Graphing:
Forgiveness, as a skill, is very difficult to define. As a training, it focuses more on resolution, retarding of hate development, and the self-benefit, rather than receiving forgiveness. The prior VSS trainings all provided skill sub-sets that can act as a foundation for a number of the VSS. In this case, optimism, empathy, and self-forgiveness are the foundation skills for forgiveness skill development. The other critical factor is how not forgiving another person is harmful to the person who does not offer forgiveness.

The forgiveness awareness skill training is separated into 3 variables. Resolution, willingness to forgive, and dislike potential turning into hate (as well as the level of openness to forgiveness). For resolution we compare the following pairs of questions. For each grouping, add up the scores (1 through 5) and determine the mean for R (Resolution).

The following questions all pertain to Resolution:
ICE Scenario 1, pt 1 : Questions 1a and 2a
ICE Scenario 2, pt 1 : Questions 1c and 2c (These 4 questions combine.)
OOCE #1 : Questions 1a and 2a (These 2 questions combine.)
ICE Scenario 1, pt 2 : Questions 1e and 2e
ICE Scenario 2, pt 2 : Questions 1g and 2g (These 4 questions combine.)
OOCE #2 : Questions 1a and 2a (These 2 questions combine.)
For these questions, if the score is lower, the participant is less likely to consider resolution.

For each of the following groupings, add up the scores (1 through 5) and determine the mean score for H (Hate):
ICE Scenario 1, pt 1 : Questions 1b and 2b
ICE Scenario 2, pt 1 : Questions 1d and 2d (These 4 questions combine.)
OOCE #1 : Questions 1b and 2b (These 2 questions combine.)

ICE Scenario 1, pt 2 : Questions 1f and 2f

ICE Scenario 2, pt 2 : Questions 1h and 2h (These 4 questions combine.)

OOCE #2 : Questions 1b and 2b (These 2 questions combine.)

The lower the combined score of these pairs indicates the participant is less likely to develop hate. The formation of hate tends to make forgiveness more difficult for people to offer.

Before determining the mean scores for forgiveness, take the answers to 3b, 3d, 3f, and 3h and invert them.

$1 = 5, 2 = 4, 3 = 3, 4 = 2, 5 = 1$

Then, add up the scores for each grouping and determine the mean scores as for resolution and hate.

The core-skill forgiveness pairs are:

ICE Scenario 1, pt 1 : Questions 3a and 3b

ICE Scenario 2, pt 1 : Questions 3c and 3d (These 4 questions combine.)

OOCE # 1 : Questions 3a and 3b (These 2 questions combine.)

ICE Scenario 1, pt 2 : Questions 3e, 4e, and 3f (These 3 questions combine.)

ICE Scenario 2, pt 2 : Questions 3g and 3h (These 2 questions combine.)

OOCE # 2 : Questions 3a and 3b (These 2 questions combine.)

OOCE # 3 : Questions 3, 4, 5, and 6 (These 4 questions combine.)

The higher the score, the greater likelihood the participant will offer or consider offering forgiveness.

ICE, Scenario 1, pt 2 the forgiveness mean adds the response of an additional question. This was done to add an element of empathy directly into the forgiveness score. This determines if the individual's forgiveness is affected by the additional information of the co-worker's personal struggles.

Appendix G

These handouts for the program did not specifically fit into another appendix.

Anger Myths:

Myth #1: Anger is not Inherited.

It is politically correct to tell people that anger is solely their fault and within their total control. Several recent studies with identical twins have shown that personality traits, such as anger, may have up to a 50% genetic component.[1] How we behave may be under our control, or can be learned to be controlled.

Myth #2: Anger Always Leads to Aggression.

A similar myth involves the misconception that the only effective way to express anger is through aggression. It is a common misconception that anger builds and escalates to the point of an aggressive outburst. Anger does not need to lead to aggression. Anger management involves incorporating a variety of behavioral strategies and self-assessment techniques to counteract this aggression.

Myth #3: People Must Be Aggressive to Achieve What They Want.

Many times people confuse aggression with assertiveness. To assertively pursue a goal (professional, personal) with a single minded determination can be seen as aggressive. The emotion of aggression is a hostile or destructive tendency or behavior.

Myth #4: Venting Anger is Always Desirable:

For many years it has been popular among mental health professionals to allow patients to release their anger in an aggressive manner. Some therapists have implemented the use of beating pillows or punching bags. We acknowledge that this is a component of Progressive Desensitization Therapy, which in the short-term has shown some effectiveness. Consistent with other research, we believe such treatment only becomes effective once the physical and verbal aggression cease. Research has found that, in the long run, people who vent their anger aggressively simply get better at being angry.[2] Simply put, venting anger in an aggressive manner usually just reinforces aggressive behavior.

Myth #5: If a Person Relapses They Have Failed.

A) Relapse refers to losing control sufficiently to dictate the need to implement a short-term strategy(s). This is a normal occurrence with any behavior that one is trying to change. A person does not fail from relapsing. A person fails by giving up or by failing to continue working on making positive changes. If a relapse should occur, have the patience and endurance to continue the therapy process, utilizing back chaining as recommended.
B) Back Sliding and Back Chaining:

Most people will "slip" when they are following a behavioral modification plan. When that happens, it is not a reason to give up on the plan. What the person should do is go back to the point in the plan (Back Chaining) where they were being successful and then begin at that point.

1. Martin E.P. Seligman, PhD, Authentic Happiness, Simon & Schuster : NY (2002), pg 47
2. Berkowitz 1970; Murray 1985; Straus, Gelles, & Steinmetz 1990

The following is the member's version of the group rules we use in our sessions.

Group Rules:

A) <u>Group Safety</u>: No violence or threats toward staff or other participants will be permitted. People only feel comfortable sharing in an environment that is perceived as a sanctuary.
B) <u>Confidentiality</u>: What happens in therapy sessions stays in therapy sessions. Some counselors may have members sign a confidentiality agreement regarding the disclosure of other members' personal information.
C) <u>In-Class and Homework Assignments</u>: Brief in-class and homework assignments will be given each week. Homework will consist of compiling a weekly assignment of the anger meter, continuing to update the Anger Control Today (ACT) sheet, and completing the various exercises that occur throughout the sessions. By completing the homework assignments, participants develop and refine individual behavioral management strategies, as well as allow more active participation in the therapy

sessions. Homework assignments provide opportunity for development and refinement. Like any type of skill development, anger management requires time and consistent practice in order to create lasting change.

D) <u>Absences and Cancellations</u>: Members must notify the group leaders in advance if they cannot attend a session. Due to the plethora of material and the way the information builds upon itself, members may not miss more than 2 of the 12 sessions. If more than 2 sessions are missed, the participant may still attend the remaining sessions, but a certificate of completion may not be issued. Participants may join another class as space becomes available. Everyone has days they just do not want to show up to something. The group leader should encourage participants to attend every session. Those potentially missed sessions are the very ones that are often the most beneficial.

E) <u>Timeout</u>: Group leaders reserve the right to call for a group timeout. A group timeout is simply defined as terminating or interrupting the discussion. If a group member feels that their anger over a certain person or subject matter is beginning to escalate out of control, they should request the group leader for a group timeout. Once a group timeout has been called, the entire group will immediately stop discussing the issue that has caused the proposed escalation. If the person whose anger has escalated simply cannot tolerate the group, they may leave the group for a cool down period, usually five to ten minutes. Once the participant feels emotionally ready, they may rejoin the group. If it is possible, such individuals should be considered for individual counseling to determine a plan of action for dealing with the triggering event. In session V, timeouts are discussed in more detail using the LEAP method. It is hoped that after session V, group participants will be able to call an individual timeout for themselves. It is also important to make sure that members do not use any timeout as a therapy avoidance technique.

Visualization Long-Term Strategy (session II):

Ideally you may record this exercise onto your phone or an audio device, playing it back when you are ready to perform the visualization. When you make the recording be sure to annunciate, speaking both slowly and evenly. Pause long enough between each sentence to give yourself sufficient time to imagine or visualize what is being said.

- Sit up or lie down comfortably
- Breathe easily
- Close your eyes

"Begin by sitting up or lying down in a comfortable position. Now close your eyes and begin breathing in an even and relaxed manner. With each inhale, allow your stomach to gently expand. With each exhale, allow it to gently contract. Continue breathing in this steady and relaxed manner.

Visualize yourself interacting with someone who angers you. Notice how you begin looking when angry, how you feel; recognize your surroundings. Visualize yourself calmly and assertively using your anger well. You know this situation is important. Use your strength to face this situation with integrity and courage. You are assertive and fair. You politely and clearly explain the end result you want. You work through the situation, listening and responding appropriately. You seek a Win/Win to No Deal solution. Together, all parties find the best solution to this problem, implementing it to the benefit of all. You are a better person from this experience. You have learned from it, and moved toward making a better future for yourself and the world. You feel refreshed and renewed at what you have accomplished."

Name_____ Age_____ Education_____
Race_____

45 Question Anger Style Probe

Check each one that applies:
1) _____I try to never get angry.
2) _____I get really nervous when others are angry.
3) _____I feel I'm doing something bad when I get angry.
4) _____I often tell people I'll do what they want, but then I forget.
5) _____I frequently say things like, "Yeah, but…" and "I'll do it later."
6) _____People tell me I must be angry but I'm not sure why.
7) _____get mad at myself a lot.
8) _____I "stuff" my anger and then get headaches, a stiff neck, stomachaches, etc.
9) _____I frequently call myself ugly names like "dummy, selfish," etc.
10)_____My anger comes on really fast.
11)_____I act before I think when I get angry.
12)_____ My anger goes away very quickly.
13)_____I get very angry when people criticize me.
14)_____People say I am easily hurt and oversensitive.
15)_____I get angry easily when I feel bad about myself.
16)_____I get mad in order to get what I want.
17)_____I try to scare others with my anger.
18)_____I sometimes pretend to be mad when I'm not really angry.
19)_____Sometimes I get angry just for the excitement or action.
20)_____I like the strong feelings that come with my anger.
21)_____Sometimes when I am bored I start arguments or pick fights.
22)_____I hang onto my anger for a long time.
23)_____I have a hard time forgiving others.
24)_____I hate people for what they've done to me.
25)_____I seem to get angry all the time.
26)_____My anger feels like a bad habit I have trouble breaking.
27)_____I get mad without thinking - it feels automatic.
28)_____I get jealous a lot, even when there is no reason.
29)_____I don't trust people very much.
30)_____Sometimes it feels like people are out to get me.

31)_____I become very angry when I defend my beliefs and opinions.

32)_____I often feel outraged about what others try to get away with.

33)_____I always know I'm right in an argument.

34)_____When things go wrong, I know it is usually my fault.

35)_____I often call myself names such as, "stupid, selfish, and idiot".

36)_____I often feel like I do not do anything right.

37)_____I have a difficult time accomplishing anything.

38)_____I am usually in relationships with people who are just not good for me.

39)_____Whenever I do anything, all I tend to notice are my mistakes.

40)_____I am always so busy I never have time to take care of myself.

41)_____I never get around to pursuing my dreams.

42)_____I am usually so busy taking care of others, that I feel like I never "catch up" on personal things.

43)_____Sometimes I hurt myself physically by scratching marks or cutting.

44)_____I take a lot of risks because I just do not care.

45)_____I am prone to accidents when I am angry.

Anger is generally expressed as either inward anger or explosive anger. It is categorized as inward (masked anger), explosive anger, and chronic anger. It can be further subdivided into various anger styles. For the purposes of this course we have chosen the eleven most prevalent and an accompanying anger probe found in the book *Letting Go Of Anger* by Dr. Efron.[18] We have modified this test and its presentation for the Group Anger Management setting. Ideally, before the first session, each member will have already taken the 45 question Anger Probe found in Appendix G. Understanding each of the anger styles can act as a beacon pointing members toward understanding the root causes of their individual anger. The questionnaire is NOT a diagnostic tool. The results are simply an indicator. It is also common for people to exhibit more than one anger type (style). Each of the 11 anger styles are covered in detail in the upcoming sessions. The questionnaire also includes the only biographical intake in the program. All of the future instruments and exercises just ask for the participant's name. This assumes that a separate and organized file is maintained of each participant.

When evaluating the probe, every three questions correlate to one of the 11 anger styles in the following questions:

1-3 Anger Avoidance
4-6 Sneaky Anger / Passive Aggressive
7-9 Anger Turned Inward
10-12 Sudden Anger
13-15 Shame-based Anger
16-18 Deliberate Anger
19-21 Excitatory Anger
22-24 Resentment / Hate
25-27 Habitual Hostility
28-30 Paranoia
31-33 Moral Anger

Questions 34-45 further subdivide anger turned inward. Anger styles rarely present themselves as neatly defined and discreet categories. They often blend together. It is quite probable that a person with anger turned inward exhibits a combination of the following inward patterns, scored as follows:

34-36 Self-blame
37-39 Self-sabotage

40-42 Self-neglect

43-45 Self-attack

Consider the first three questions of the probe:

1) I try never to get angry.
2) I get really nervous when others are angry.
3) I feel I'm doing something bad when I get angry.

If a person answered "yes" on one or two of the above questions, they exhibit some signs of the anger avoidance anger style. Encourage them to pay special attention when that anger style is discussed during group therapy. They may also record it in their ACT sheet. If a person answered "yes" to all three questions, have them record "Anger Avoidance" on their ACT and encourage them to pay special attention when that anger style is discussed in the upcoming sessions. In the case of questions 34-45, they all deal with some aspect of anger turned inward. There is no objective number of yes's a person must score before one can definitely say they are dealing with a particular sub-category of anger turned inward. Look for patterns in this probe that correlate with other observed behaviors in order to adjust the short and long-term strategies used by members in their Anger Control Today (ACT) plan.

"Worst Day Ever?"

by Chanie Gorki

Today was the absolute worst day ever
And don't try to convince me that
There's something good in every day
Because, when you take a closer look,
This world is a pretty evil place.
Even if
Some goodness does shine through once in a while
Satisfaction and happiness don't last.
And it's not true that
It's all in the mind and heart
Because
True happiness can be obtained
Only if one's surroundings are good
It's not true that good exists
I'm sure you can agree that
the reality
Creates
My attitude
It's all beyond my control
and you'll never in a million years hear me say that
Today was a good day

(Now read the poem from bottom to top)

Appendix M

Music

The following is the handout for the criteria and the genres of suggested music:

For those dealing with anger issues, consider the following suggestions in your music listening selections.

Do the following:

- Only listen to music with positive lyrics and themes, or no lyrics.
- Choose slow to moderate music, around 60 beats per minute (tempo). For most people slow music tends to calm them. For a minority of people, fast music calms them instead. Therefore, carefully consider what style calms you when selecting music for your own individual anger management, while keeping the music positive.
- Do not listen to excessively loud music
- Do not listen to angry or aggressive music.
- Do not listen to music with negative lyrics.
- Consider listening to slower, easier speed music.

The following music and genres all have songs that fit the above criteria:

Jazz, Classical, Religious, Opera, Nature Sounds, Meditation Music, Love Songs, Hymns, Chants, Cultural such as Native American or Aboriginal, Soft Rock, Easy Listening and instrumental such as Mandolin, Harp, or Flute.

Listening to music that follows these criteria has many benefits. An abundance of scientific studies list these benefits and help explain why we have chosen these types of music. For those interested in this information, it is included here:

Almost everyone knows that music affects emotions. Historically, there was little scientific evidence to prove this point. This is probably why almost no one mentions it in books on anger management or includes music in their program. But in your gut, you know that some music makes you sad and other music makes you feel pleasant, thoughtful, or even calms you down. As far back as the 5th century B.C., Pythagoras had music played at his university in Crotona to influence the students. Music was selected in the morning to help make them more attentive, and music was chosen in the evening to help students relax and sleep.[30] He was no dummy, and as you probably know, the Pythagorean Theorem was named after him.

In the early 18th century, King Georg I of England commissioned the famous composer George Frederick Handel to compose music to treat his condition of stress and memory loss.[31] King George had gotten the idea from the Biblical account by King Saul (1 Samuel 16:23) who had also dealt with similar problems by using music. Handel composed his Water Music for the task. It is still used today in music therapy to calm and relax patients. There are many more examples throughout history of intelligent, educated, and well respected people using music to treat emotional problems and various ailments.

There are many examples in more modern times as well, and the evidence is beginning to stack. In the early 1940's the Muzak Corporation ran an experiment playing music several times throughout the day in an attempt to improve production and attentiveness in the workplace.[32] In the study they used slower, tranquil music. This had the opposite effect, actually lowering productivity when played continuously throughout the day. Muzak Corporation eventually designed elevator and office music, finding that the easy listening music calmed people down and reduced apprehension.

Perhaps you have heard stories of music helping plants to grow. There are many studies in this area, but they are by no means conclusive. Some studies show that violent and aggressive music harms plants or stunts their growth. Other studies show that any music helps plants grow. The majority of the studies suggest that certain music helps plants grow, and other types of music seem to hinder plant growth. One study showed that roses grew better with positive and religious music, and grew poorly with music such as "Bringer of Storms" by Hate Eternal.[33] Another study, published in *Popular Mechanics*, showed that corn grew better with music.[34] We have chosen music for the program that falls in line with the general trend of these and similar plant studies.

We also researched and reviewed studies regarding water crystals and the effects of music. In the 1990's, Dr. Emoto performed experiments making ice crystals with water exposed to various things such as sound, pollution, or words.[35]

He found that under certain conditions, water will form asymmetrical and unpleasant looking ice crystals. Among the conditions that caused this were negative or violent music. In contrast, pleasant music and sounds would create appealing and symmetrical ice crystals. We know our own bodies are made of 76% water, and that we carry millions of tiny crystals within our bones and brain.[36] Though it is by no means conclusive, if Dr. Emoto's work is correct, the influence negative music has upon water may also apply to people.

Music has been shown to affect animals as well. It can help cows produce more milk,[37] and hens to lay more eggs.[38] Even little lab rats seem to show a preference for Bach over hard rock music.[39] Loud music can take a raw egg and make it hard boiled.[40] Putting a protein in a liquid and exposing it to high pitched sound causes it to coagulate.[41] The assumption being that certain high pitched music would do the same to your organs and blood. Loud music is also believed to create free radicals in people.[42] Free radicals can destroy tissues leading to impairment, disease, and accelerated aging.

We now know that music directly affects people in many other ways as well. Hard rock, heavy metal, and rap music have adverse effects on EEG patterns.[43] Heavy metal music has been shown to increase feelings of tension and nervousness, a problem for those dealing with anger.[44] One study cited that loud music, regardless of genre, tended to agitate most people[45] Another showed that exposure to songs with violent lyrics is sufficient to alter mood and increase aggression.[46]

Studies show similar findings in children as well. One showed that kids who listened to heavy metal music, regardless of the words, were angrier than children who were given "easy listening" music. The heavy metal group also scored as having more negative attitudes toward women, despite the words of the music being unintelligible to the children.[47] One study showed that babies as old as 8 months can discern angry musical tones.[48] If these negative lyrics and aggressive music do indeed create tension, anxiety, and anger in people, then they probably have long-term negative effects. We know that long-term stress and anger tend to negatively affect health, emotional well-being, and relationships. If the data is correct, people should avoid music with:

- Negative Lyrics
- Violent Content
- Excessive Volume

Some neuroscientists say that the brain does not appear to distinguish a thought from an event. By some measurement standards, thinking about things can create the same response in your brain as doing those same things. Simultaneously we know that emotions can trigger both thoughts and memories. If these are all true, we can postulate that things that stimulate emotion, such as music, can cause us to experience both positive and negative mental states. According to the research we have gathered, just like negative music, positive music has many effects on people. Music with positive themes, lyrics, and soothing sounds can do the following:

- It can reduce stress, pain, and anxiety.[49]
- It activates parts of the brain related to movement, attention, planning, and memory.[50]
- Students score higher on tests after listening to Mozart.[51] This study was performed at the University of California Irvine. This result is now referred to as "The Mozart Effect".
- Classical Baroque music (Europe from 1550 to 1700 AD) increases learning potential by as much as five times.[52]
- Baroque music is used to teach foreign languages much more quickly.[53]
- Slow Jazz, Classical, and positive music improves test scores and IQ scores.[54]
- Slow, positive music lowers heart rate, blood pressure, reduces breathing rates, changes the skin's electrical resistance, and dilates the pupils.[55]
- Relaxing music lowers cortisol and immunoglobin A amounts in the blood, boosting immune function.[56]
- Music during an event can augment emotions.[57] For instance, certain music at funerals enhances sadness.
- Soothing music helps both infants and their mothers to sleep better and reduce anxiety.[58]
- It is used to help calm the elderly.[59]
- It smooths out brain waves and synchronizes the left and right sides of the brain.[60] This is interesting because long periods of meditation seem to produce the same results.[61]

In order for music to affect people in so many different ways, it would have to affect more than just the part of the brain that picks up sound. Studies using PET scans show exactly that. Music also affects parts of the brain that are considered subconscious areas,[62] and areas associated with emotions and hormones.[63] Some of the brain's neural pathways for music also coincide with activating memory.[64] The combined data of all the studies tell us that the proper music can affect you unconsciously, especially in regulating and influencing emotion. For this reason we feel positive music belongs as part of a comprehensive anger management treatment plan.

There are many counter arguments to the music suggestions we make. One of the most prevalent is that people will sometimes say that some of this "supposed" negative music is music they actually enjoy. For instance, after an argument some people may listen to something fast and aggressive, like speed metal. For these people, aggressive or fast music may actually calm them down as they find it placating or comforting.[65] Though some of this music may calm them down, research still shows that you should avoid negative messages and lyrics.[66] The music recommendations we have made are based on what affects most people, especially in regard to emotions such as anger and anxiety. It makes sense to listen to music that is calming and has positive lyrics, especially in helping with any anger issues you might have.

In the beginning of this appendix we gave many examples of potentially beneficial music. We recommended slow or moderate tempo music. This is because music can cause your heart rate to speed up or slow down closer in time with the music.[67] If you want to get technical, research suggests you listen to music around 60 beats per minute or slower when you specifically want to calm down. Faster paced positive music still has the other benefits listed in this appendix, so do not mechanically select music all the same, slow tempo. Following are some specific examples of songs that fit our suggested criteria, arranged by genre. Keep in mind this list is tiny compared to the possibilities. Do your own research and you will find many songs that you enjoy and fit your anger management goals.

Jazz:
"Europa" by various artists, including Santana
"Il N'y Pas D'Amour Heureux" by Nina Simone

Christian:
"I Can Only Imagine" by MercyME
"Forgiveness" by Mathew West

Classical:
"Fur Elise" Opus No. 25 by Beethoven
"Symphony #40" by Mozart
"Carmina Burana" by Carl Orff
"Opus #299 for Flute and Harp" by Mozart

Opera:
"Santa Lucia" by Andrea Bocelli
"O Sole Mio" by Luciano Pavarotti

Hymns:
"Holy, Holy, Holy" by the Mormon Tabernacle Choir and Orchestra
"How Great Thou Art" by Hymns Triumphant Performers and Symphony
"Invitatoire: Ecce Venit" by the Benedictine Monks of Notre-Dame

Love Songs:
"Unforgettable" by Nat King Cole
"The Way You Look Tonight" by Tony Bennet
"Say Something" by a Great Big World and Christina Aguilera

Meditation Music (New Wave)
"Music for Brainwave Massage" by Dr. Jeffrey Thompson

Nature Sounds:
Rain
Ocean Waves

Uncategorized Positive Music:
"Deora Ar Mo Chroi" by Enya

Appendix N

Nutrition

In relation to anger management, nutrition is important. Poor nutrition may have the following negative consequences:

- Depression, anxiety, irritability, tiredness, agitation, and mood swings.
- Reduced immune function, more sickness, and longer recovery.
- It may impact job performance and keep you from earning a sufficient lifestyle.
- It can diminish your sex life.
- It may damage your social relationships.

All of these consequences can make anger problems worse. Some of them can also relate to your individual anger triggers and make you more likely to react to them.

By contrast, good nutrition may have the following benefits:

- It improves immune function, reducing sickness and helping happiness.
- It gives you more energy allowing you to accomplish more.
- It can improve your sex life.
- It helps regulate brain chemistry, improving mood and making your emotionally resilient.
- By improving mood it can enrich your social relationships.

All of these benefits can help improve your happiness, reduce your stress, and make you less likely to react to anger triggers. For all of these reasons, good nutrition is important to any anger management program.

The following is a condensed list of nutritional recommendations:

1. If possible, predominately eat whole foods such as nuts, grains, fruits, vegetables, fish, cheese, and meat.
2. Avoid the following: processed foods, refined sugar, tobacco, artificial sweeteners, saturated fats, and drugs.

3. Consume in moderation or caution: caffeine, alcohol, and table salt.
4. Follow the restrictions of your doctor, such as those with gout consuming less meat and cheese.
5. Get sufficient sleep. Lack of sleep can cause irritability and negatively affect your health. For most adults sufficient sleep is about 6 to 8 hours per night.

It is recommended that members educate themselves further in regards to proper nutrition. There is a plethora of current work on the subject. The rest of appendix N is dedicated to those who are interested in a more detailed discussion on our nutritional recommendations. All of these recommendations are made because of the effect they potentially have on mood and anger management.

We all know diet is important, but we often forget exactly why. Among other things, our diet has the ability to affect the hormone, neurotransmitter, and chemical catalyst levels in our bodies and brains. All of these have the ability to affect our mood, and to change the way we feel and behave. Nutrition is so important to mental health that it has been said that nutritional deficiencies are the root of many mental imbalances.[68] Conditions such as insomnia, fatigue, irritability, poor concentration, weight loss, and weight gain can all be regulated or corrected with proper nutrition. Each of these symptoms is listed as a possible characteristic associated with chronic depression, and can also appear in conjunction with some of the anger styles discussed in the program. Any one of these symptoms can impair with your ability to handle anger situations.

Take for example blood sugar. Too many simple carbohydrates (carbs) and sugars cause your blood sugar levels to rise. Then your pancreas dumps insulin to digest it. The spike in blood levels of insulin can lead to hazy thinking and drowsiness. Reduced concentration then follows once the blood sugar begins to drop too low from the extra insulin. Not taking in enough or the right type of carbs, such as a "low carb" diet, can cause problems as well. If your blood sugar levels fall too low you may get weak, irritable, anxious, and in some cases angry. Snickers ran an ad campaign telling people they are "not themselves" when hungry. Low blood sugar levels can lead to reductions in brain serotonin levels. Low serotonin levels (the primary inhibitory neurotransmitter) can cause irritability, reduced sleep, migraines, anxiety, and depression. Each of these symptoms can aggravate an existing anger issue.

I. Deficiencies.

They can affect your mood and exacerbate anger issues. If you are deficient in:

A) The eight essential B-vitamins, it inhibits neurotransmitter production, causing anxiety and depression.
B) Magnesium, it can cause insomnia, anxiety, and nervousness.
C) In chromium, it causes unstable blood sugar levels, resulting in mood swings and the problems associated with blood sugar.
D) In beneficial fats, such as Omega-3 and Omega-6, it can cause mood swings and cognitive problems. The brain is composed of about 2/3 fat.

II. Things to Avoid.

All of the following things can worsen mood, exacerbating anger problems. Avoid or eliminate:

A) Recreational drugs.
B) Tobacco products.
C) Artificial foods. This includes artificial sweeteners, fake butter, and artificial cheeses.
D) Fried Foods. Lightly fried foods in the proper oils are all right. The proper oils are discussed later.
E) Trans fatty acids (hydrogenated fats or saturated fats). Absorbed by the brain, these contribute to anxiety, depression, and produce toxins when digested.
F) Chemical food additives. This includes excitoxins such as MSG or aspartame, which destroy neurons and contribute to depression, anxiety, and restlessness.
G) Cotton seed oil. It is unhealthy compared to more traditional oils, such as olive.
H) White flour, white rice, and/or processed foods. They are less healthy than their whole food counterparts.
I) Table sugar (sucrose). Linked to depression, excessive sugar consumption can increase cortisol (a sign of stress) in the blood, disturb sleep, and deplete B-vitamins.
J) Personal food allergies. They can aggravate both depression and anxiety. If you suspect you have a food allergy, and want to test it, you can take the Coca Pulse Test.[69] It is possible your heartrate increases for other reasons, giving you a false positive. You will want to perform the test on a given food multiple times in order to be sure. Perform the test as follows:

1. Before eating a suspected food allergen, take your resting pulse rate.
2. Place a bite of the suspected food allergen on your tongue for 30 seconds.
3. Recheck your pulse.
4. If your pulse rate goes up by more than six beats per minute, it indicates an allergy or sensitivity to that food.

K) Drug interactions. If you take two or more medicines, check with your doctor(s) to ensure there are no negative chemical interactions.

III. Things Consumed in Moderation.

That covers all the "do not's". Consume the following in moderation:

A) Meat. Excessive consumption can raise your bad (LDL) cholesterol level, saturated fat level, and risk for some cancers.
B) Caffeine. This includes coffee, black tea, and many soft drinks. It is arguable that coffee has benefits, such as reduced chance of Alzheimer's, lower rate of diabetes, and is an antioxidant. In excessive amounts, coffee consumption reduces B-vitamins, causing anxiety, depression, sleep disturbance, and increased cortisol in the blood. Limit yourself to a reasonable amount of coffee. We suggest no more than 3 cups a day. Green tea is a great replacement for coffee with many of the same reported benefits, and more; and only 1/6 the caffeine per cup.
C) Alcohol. Drink responsibly and in moderation. Beer and wine seem to have more benefits than heavier proof alcohols.
D) Salt (NaCl). The suggested intake amount of salt is about 2 grams (2000 mg) per day. The average American diet is almost four times that number. Most people do not need to ever add ANY salt to their diet. There are salt substitutes, such as "No Salt" that use potassium chloride (KCl) instead of table salt. If you consistently add salt to your food, use this substitute instead. Also consider cooking with organic sea salt as it also has trace minerals compared to normal table salt.
E) Genetically Modified Foods (GMO's). GMO plants tend to be hardier and more resistant. As a result, they can tolerate and are exposed to higher levels of pesticides. This is one of the reasons to avoid GMO foods.

IV. Recommendations.

Organic vs. Non-organic.

Organic fruits and vegetables tend to have less chemical toxins than non-organic. They also pass the 1000 year test that goes like this: "If people ate that type of food 1000 years ago, it is probably all right to eat the same type today". Foods such as beer, wine, or eggs have been eaten for millennia. As such there are no known bad health effects of consuming them in moderation. Things such as aspartame, DDT, or cotton seed oil were not consumed a 1000 years ago, and should be avoided.

When selecting a diet, we recommend a (not so strict) vegetarian diet. Vegetarian diets:

- Keep people slimmer.
- Reduce your chances of heart disease, diabetes, some cancers, and dementia.
- Help with blood pressure problems.
- Elevate mood (in cases of previously improper nutrition).
- Provide a broad range of micro and trace nutrients.
- Provide more fiber, more antioxidants, and more vitamins than high meat diets.

Consider adding in about 5 servings of fish a week into a vegetarian diet. By eating some fish you are less likely to develop macular (eye) degeneration [70] or Alzheimer's [71]. People who eat at least two servings of fish per week perform better on a wide range of cognitive tests.[72] Fish such as salmon, tuna, mackerel, sardine, herring, and lake trout all carry favorable amounts of fatty acids.

The proper cooking oils are also important. Read the labels and only purchase oils high in unsaturated fats. Extra virgin, cold pressed oils are preferred.

- For low temperature cooking use: avocado, safflower, sunflower, or flaxseed oil.
- For moderate temperature cooking use olive oil.
- For high temperature cooking consider using oils of sesame, palm kernel, coconut, or organic ghee.

V. Supplements.

When eating a (not so strict) vegetarian diet, some people need to consider supplements. Be careful to consume only the recommended amounts. Do not add unnecessary supplements to your diet if you are getting enough of the supplement naturally. Too much of anything can be harmful.

Suggested Supplements:

A) Blue-green algae and algae products such as Spirulina:

These are highly nutritious super-foods, even containing some Omega-3 DHA. A couple of tablespoons a day is enough for most adults.

B) Plant or whey based protein powder:

Important to muscle building vegetarians, it is a standard supplement. It has most of the benefits of a steak without animal hormones, LDL cholesterol, and mutagens.

C) Omega-3 fatty acids:

If you do not consume enough fish or meat products, you may need to supplement with Omega-3's. Some doctors recommend a blend of EPA and DHA Omega-3's.[73] A diet containing sufficient amounts of Omega-3's is linked to lower incidence of cancer, asthma, depression, ADHD, and rheumatoid arthritis. It also supports healthy heart function, cell activity, retina development, and healthy brain function.

VI. Suggested Reading:

For those serious about a balanced (not so strict) vegetarian diet, it requires a certain amount of self-education. The rough draft of this book included a complete dietary plan. That plan, with all its calculations, became too wieldy for an anger management book. Here are some resources on this subject:

- www.lef.org. They provide current research on supplements. They are a for-profit organization, but their positions are backed up by research.
- www.chooseveg.com
- www.bbcgoodfood.com/howto/guide/balanced-diet-vegetarian
- www.peta.org. This is an animal rights organization, but their vegetarian information is excellent.

Appendix P

Positive Thinking and Speech

"As a man thinks in his heart, so is he". (King Solomon, Proverbs 3:27)

Ever since the invention of clocks and races, people have recorded how fast they run. No one ever ran a mile in less than four minutes. In the early 1950's it was medical opinion that no human could run that fast. Articles appeared in medical journals claiming it was physically impossible. It was called a barrier and many runners considered it impenetrable. Some people even warned that runners training to break the barrier might die trying. One medical doctor who refused to believe these ideas was Roger Bannister. He eventually became knighted, because in 1954 he exploded past the finish line with a time of 3:59.4, becoming the first runner to break through the mythical barrier.

What happened next is even more amazing. Since time memorial, and the invention of the stop watch, no one has ever broken the four minute barrier. So did it take another 60 years for some unusual person to come along and perform the same feat? Actually it took a few months. By the end of twelve months, four other runners broke the same "impenetrable" barrier. Some have argued that techniques and nutrition among runners just got better in 1954. But there is no clear data that supports this. What we do know is that with 3:59.4 minutes, an idea changed. People learned that it could be done. Thought and reality might be related, and many studies suggest this.

There was a university study where the 1953 graduating class was asked about their goals. According to the study, only three percent of the graduates had written down clear, specific goals for themselves. Twenty years later, those same three percent had accumulated more financial worth than the entire remaining 97%, and also reported greater life satisfaction.[74] This thought-reality connection also works in the training of skills.

In one study, seventy-two players, from eight college basketball teams, practiced relaxation and visualization techniques. They imagined themselves throwing perfect foul shots, picturing it in entirety. Their shooting averages soon improved by seven percent - a change so significant the coaches reported the improved shooting produced eight additional wins during the season.[75] In this same study the athletes were hooked up to sensors that measured their neuromuscular activity during the mental training. It showed that the same muscles used in free-throw shooting were activated during the practice of imagery. Subtly, their bodies were going through the same motions as if they were actually performing the free-throws.

A similar study was done at the Olympic Training Center in Colorado with thirty college-age golfers. The golfers visualized sinking perfect putts. After one week the relaxation and visualization training group improved their putting accuracy by 30 percent. The group that trained without visualization only improved by 11 percent.[76] One study involving weight lifters showed that visualization led to bigger muscles and more weight gain compared to those who did not.[77] Former Governor Arnold Schwarzenegger used to visualize his muscles getting bigger during his workouts. As part of his body building routine, it helped propel him to the pinnacle of body building competitions, becoming a multiple time Mr. Olympia winner.

The evidence from sports training is so broad, that some researchers have concluded that the central nervous system does not distinguish between real and imagined events.[78] If imagining movements causes muscles to activate in much the same way as if you were actually performing the action, and if it improves your skill in that activity, it places profound importance on the things you visualize or imagine. Visualizing things that are generally positive might train you to respond in positive ways. We would expect the opposite to hold true for visualizing negative things. It might also explain why people who use venting in regards to anger actually end up "rehearsing" it, becoming angrier.

In recent times there are also many studies showing an interaction between our thinking and computers generating random numbers. These studies generate so many random numbers in the experiments, that it is hard to refute their statistical significance. Something is happening, even if we do not know the exact relation. A famous example is the Princeton EGGS experiments.[79] In this study subjects sit near a device that makes random numbers. They have no physical contact with it. They are then asked to make the device produce higher or lower numbers. The experiments show that thinking somehow interacts with the machines, skewing the results enough to not be "random".

There are many such machines linked together around the world. Princeton runs this ongoing experiment in conjunction with the Institute of Noetic Sciences. They have published data claiming that at the time of major world events the random number generators create "peaks of order". They are claiming that human consciousness (as a whole) may have a broad effect on physical events.[80]

Outside of science and experiments, many people believe there is a relationship between thinking and reality. Consider the following quotes:

"Our life always expresses the result of our dominant thoughts." - Soren Kierkegaard

"Once you replace negative thoughts with positive ones, you'll start having positive results." - Willie Nelson

"We are shaped by our thoughts; we become what we think. When the mind is pure, joy follows like a shadow that never leaves." - Buddha

"All action results from thought, so it is thoughts that matter." - Sai Baba

"Our life is what our thoughts make it." - Marcus Aurelius

"Your beliefs become your thoughts, your thoughts become your words, your words become your actions, your actions become your habits, your habits become your values, your values become your destiny" - Mahatma Gandhi

"Some people keep God in a Sunday morning box and say, 'Hey, I did my religious duty.' That's fine, but the scripture says to pray without ceasing. And I think that means all through the day you're talking to God. Even if it's in your thoughts." - Joel Osteen

The preceding list includes a diverse group of people, from a country singer to a country leader. Yet they are all saying essentially the same thing, your thoughts and words have an effect on your future. Knowing this is one thing, but implementing it in a practical way can be difficult. In this course, whenever practical, we presented information in a positive way. We used positive affirmations as part of the therapy, and where applicable removed any negative language. The VSS training, such as optimism, has the effect of developing perspective and positive thinking (through counter arguments) in a progressive, step by step fashion.

Most popular works are scant in giving practical, step by step instructions for transforming your thinking. Even best-selling books on the subject say things like, "use positive words when talking with others", without explaining how you change your behaviors. That is the equivalent of telling an alcoholic, "Quit drinking and your problem will be solved". Many professional works engage in this same "Osmosis Therapy". They repeat information on what should be changed without clear explanation on how to change it and keep it changed. The prevalent idea seems to be that if you repeat the "whats" long enough, people will eventually figure out which "hows" work for them. Osmosis therapy still has value by continually immersing people in positive information.

Below is a list of some additional resources regarding the power of thoughts and words:

- *The Power of Positive Thinking* by Remez Sasson
- *The Secret* by Rhonda Byrne
- *7 Habits of Highly Effective People* by Steven R. Covey
- training.tonyrobbins.com Helpful information on Transformation Vocabulary, The Power of Words, Positive Thoughts
- www.joelosteen.com
- www.successconsciousness.com/index_000009.htm has information regarding positive affirmations
- http://media.noetic.org
- http://noosphere.princeton.edu

Appendix S

Morals, Ethics, Philosophy

There is a species so mean hearted that the strong just take from the weak, and emotions rule their day. Contracts have no value, and neighbors will fight one another over land rights. The most ruthless are often in charge, sitting at the top of the social ladder and negotiating with force. In extreme cases they are even capable of cannibalism. I am sure you have guessed the name of this species, it is the baboon.

Yeah...these guys again. Though they may not be on our level when it comes to wine sipping, they certainly have some very human characteristics. The baboons in charge really do get frustrated, but their solution is to beat up the weaker guys. Those guys in turn will find someone smaller or weaker than them to hit. They can be quite vicious. But as we stated earlier, not all troops run the same. Our special troop from the intro has no courts, no written laws, and no churches. Yet they still have a sense of what is acceptable in their society and what is "verboten". The group as a whole knows which behaviors need correction. This is not so remarkable as many animal societies do the same thing; they define their societal morality. The same goes for us. Even if we don't all agree, morals are something most people understand.

In the intro we said that many psychologists have mentioned the importance of morals, such as Freud, Rogers, and Jung. There is also a growing movement among some classically trained counselors to discuss moral issues in the context of their therapy. In the US some of the most prevalent among these are Christian Counselors. In regard to the value of morals, it is as if everyone is saying the same thing, "we should look at this thing". Yet it seems that most are unwilling to publicly walk out onto the ledge and openly discuss the point. We feel a discussion on morality is of such benefit to those dealing with anger issues, that to exclude it from our program would be reckless.

Morals are commonly defined as principles or habits in respect to right or wrong conduct. They refer to the generally accepted customs of proper living and behavior within a society. Morals usually involve the bigger questions and are defined by custom, religion, and societal agreement. They are often confused with ethics. For the sake of clarity, ethics regard the standards of honest and honorable dealings and methods of practice. They most commonly apply to professions or businesses, such as the standards of conduct prescribed for physicians or therapists. Things regarding integrity and honesty tend to fall within both categories.

Discussed in chapter 1, the six core virtues are built upon morals. Each individual culture may define morals differently. The virtues a culture holds in high regard are derived from their moral beliefs. Surprisingly, across many diverse cultures and over millennia, the same six virtues are repeatedly counted among the exemplars of right conduct. It cannot be coincidence that almost every society, culture, religion, and philosophy have picked the same virtues among their core values.[81] It stands to reason that various societies promote moral codes that keep their society functioning. It would be a form of cultural suicide to allow people to kill their neighbors after an argument. In such a way, extremely unhealthy morals could ruin a society. It is therefore no surprise that the same good morals keep appearing across so many different cultures. They are necessary, and most people learn them at a very young age.

There is evidence that even infants have some understanding of right and wrong. In one study the psychologists, using stuffed animals, would present toddlers and infants with short play. One of the stuffed animals would either beat up the other one, or steal some item, or commit other negative behaviors. Regardless of which stuffed animal was used to be the "mean one", toddlers consistently chose to play with the "nicer one". The conclusion of this study implied that children less than a year old have some concept of right and wrong behavior.[82]

Our first moral lessons usually regard these concepts of right and wrong, including such topics as sharing, stealing, or harming. Those lessons are usually not, "Don't steal because you might get caught or go to jail". When children ask their parents why they should have certain morals, parents often respond with, "It is the right thing to do". As adults, from a certain point of view it does not matter if we believe in these morals or not. It does however matter if we live by them.

If you live in a society and there is some agreement on proper moral conduct, it benefits everyone. If both you and society live by a similar moral code:

- You reduce your aggressive opportunities and are less likely to create conflict.
- More people will be in agreement and there will be less aggression within the society.
- Your stress will be reduced because you need not make as many moral decisions.

- You will attract and interact with like-minded individuals.
- You will have a more positive outlook.

All of these reasons combine to improve your social relationships, making you healthier and happier psychologically.

Morals are discussed in each of the anger management sessions and correspond to that particular session's anger style(s). Each of the morals, if incorporated, are designed to minimize anger episodes. If you want to effectively incorporate some of the morals into whatever long-term strategy (LTS) you are using for your anger, consider the following:

There is no single step by step process for incorporating the various morals into the long-term strategies. If you are to use or experience anger, make it constructive. Such anger begins by considering if the episode will eventually hurt yourself or someone else. When you are angry or encountering your anger cues ask, "What are you getting angry for?" Is it to enforce your will on others? Is it you do not want to consider that you might be wrong? When you're thinking about the moral issues, consider the baboons. Should you act against your or society's moral code to entertain your anger?

Appendix Y

Yoga

"If I'm losing balance in a pose, I stretch higher and God reaches down to steady me. It works every time, and not just in yoga." -Sri Krishna Pattahbi Jois, founder of modern Ashtanga Yoga

In this appendix we explain the following:

- Diaphragmatic Breathing
- Seated Yogic Exercise Routine
- Progressive Muscle Relaxation

Diaphragmatic Breathing (Belly Breathing aka "Back to Childhood Breathing"):

A generalized strategy for calming and dealing with all types of anger is slow, deep breathing known as diaphragmatic breathing. When breathing, the inhales and the exhales are for an equal amount of time. If you are alone and meditating, you might be able to hear your own heartbeat. If you develop the skill of hearing it as you breathe, you can inhale and exhale for an equal number of heartbeats. The breathing is performed with the eyes closed. It may also be used during the seated yoga exercises or as a short-term calming technique. In situations where it is used for calming, it may not be appropriate to close your eyes. It is generally performed with the hands folded gently on the lap (some schools of meditation will advise on particular hand gestures). Experienced practitioners could modify this technique according to their own understanding or their teacher's advice.

Begin by sitting up straight, comfortable and relaxed. Lightly place the tip of the tongue at the top of the mouth, between the hard and soft palette. If possible, only breathe through the nose during the exercise. Always complete the breathing cycle by finishing on an exhale. Expel the air from the lungs, beginning the exercise on the inhale.

In order to get the feel for breathing diaphragmatically, place one hand lightly on your upper chest and the other onto your belly. Now softly take a breath through your nose, allowing the air to fill up the lungs from bottom to top. The hand on your belly will move out as the belly expands outward and will move back as the belly contracts. The hand on your chest should not move until the top of the lungs begin to fill. Continue to breathe slowly, steadily, and evenly, with the inhale and exhale equal. The breath should feel calm, smooth, and relaxed.

In yoga, there are dozens of different breathing exercises with hundreds of publically known variations. For those interested on further reading in this subject we have included a list of resources at the end of this appendix.

Yoga Seated Exercise:

Performed at the end of each session, yoga is an adjunctive LTS. We recommend it because it is easy to perform, has many health benefits, and can be practiced almost anywhere. References regarding yoga's benefits are listed at the end of this appendix along with further suggested reading.

Before beginning, observe these simple suggestions:

- Ensure clothing is unrestrictive and comfortable. If necessary, it is appropriate to remove restrictive clothing such as jackets or loosen items such as belts.
- If possible, breathe through the nose the entire time.
- Use diaphragmatic breathing during the exercises.
- Keep the tongue placed at the roof of the mouth, between the hard and soft palate.
- Only perform maneuvers that feel both comfortable and safe.
- Stop performing any maneuver if you feel dizziness, spotty vision, or shortness of breath.

The following is a seated stretching routine. This sequence of six moves can be completed in five to seven minutes. It can be performed by anyone able to move their arms and neck while seated. Each move flows into the next. The order of the moves is such that it promotes relaxation, with the brisker moves performed toward the end of the sequence. The last move (the Palm Flex) is designed to be performed slowly, with the breathing slow and focused. Performed in this manner, the sequence will relax the body and calm the mind.

1. Sitting Deep Breathing:

   This move is performed in two parts, using the diaphragmatic breathing. Begin by interlocking the fingers under the chin with the palms facing down, and the elbows facing out at shoulder height. Keep the chin parallel to the floor while inhaling and raising the elbows as high as possible. Once the inhale is completed and the elbows are raised as high as possible, exhale while lowering the elbows back down to where they touch the front of the chest. Simultaneously push up the chin with the back of the interlocked fingers. The hands will form a single fist with the gaze directed upward. The pressure on the chin should be mild as you create a gentle stretch on the back of the neck.

2. Circular Neck Rotations:

    Sit upright. Continue to touch the tongue to the roof of the mouth. Rotate the neck in an oval pattern. One revolution should include both an inhale and an exhale. Because of the mechanics of the neck, it is safe to bring the head far forward, almost touching the chin to the upper chest. Due to the risk of injury, do not extend the head back as far as it will go during the rotation. This will cause the loop that the head travels to be oval shaped and more forward than back. After completing about seven revolutions in one direction, complete seven in the other. Both sides combined should take no more than a minute to complete.

3. Seated Upward Salute:

    Place your hands above your head and interlock the fingers. While keeping the fingers interlocked, rotate the palms upward, facing the ceiling. Extend the arms as high as possible. Feel as if the spine is lengthening. If it feels comfortable, you may look up at the ceiling while performing the stretch. Otherwise, continue keeping the gaze forward and the neck relaxed. Be careful to maintain your balance in the chair, avoiding leaning backward. Maintain this posture for four complete breathes or about twenty seconds.

4. Bent Arm Crosses:

    First, ensure there is sufficient space between people in order to safely complete this exercise. Sit up straight and keep the gaze forward. Pay special attention to maintaining the neck and head relaxed during the exercise. Form both hands into light and relaxed fists, palms facing down, with both elbows kept at the height of the shoulders. While keeping the arms bent, push the elbows back as far as they will comfortably go. This motion is done with a small amount of speed, creating a light and gentle bounce. Kicking the elbows back in this fashion will lightly stretch the chest and shoulders. On each repetition, alternate crossing one wrist over the other, with both wrists and palms continuing to face the floor. Diaphragmatic breathing is not used in this exercise. Rather, the emphasis is on coordinating a short, light exhale with the backward kicking of the elbows. The breathing is more vigorous than with diaphragmatic breathing. Perform a total of fourteen to twenty repetitions. This should take less than thirty seconds to complete.

5. Seated Twisting with Heart Hands:

    Place your feet solidly on the floor with your spine erect. Put your palms together with both of your thumbs touching the chest. Keep a small space between the palms as if you were holding something precious between them. Raise your elbows to a comfortable height, close to the height of your wrists and inhale. While maintaining this position, rotate your torso as far as you can to the left while exhaling. Inhale back to the center. Then exhale while rotating as far as you can to the right, keeping the spine erect and the hands over the chest. This is one repetition. Continue breathing diaphragmatically, completing up to ten full repetitions.

6. Palm Flex:

    Place the hands comfortably on the knees with the palms facing upward, toward the ceiling. Using diaphragmatic breathing, fully open your hands stretching the palms as you inhale. Lightly close the hand, making a soft fist as you exhale. Be sure to feel the hand only lightly flexed on the exhale. This move helps counteract some of the physical tension in the hands. Do ten repetitions being sure to coordinate the movement with the diaphragmatic breathing.

Progressive Relaxation Exercise.

The following progressive relaxation is intended to be recorded, with the audio played back during relaxation. Read aloud all of the words as written, except for the pauses which are contained in << >>. One breath cycle is a complete inhale and a complete exhale. Record and read aloud the following:

"If sitting, place your hands on your thighs. If lying down, place your arms to the side, palms up. Close your eyes, relax your face and shoulders, and place the tongue at the roof of your mouth, between your hard and soft palate. Begin by focusing on and being aware of your breathing. As you inhale through the nose, allow your abdomen to gently expand, filling your lungs to about 3/4. As you exhale, gently contract the abdomen. Make the amount of time that you inhale and exhale equal. Begin taking a slight pause between your inhales and exhales. Keep this pause between breaths about a second long. Each combined inhale and exhale is a breath cycle. Gently lengthen the inhale and exhale a few times while still keeping them equal in length. <<pause for about 30 seconds>>

As you continue breathing deeply, gently, and smoothly, slowly inhale and clench your fists tightly. Hold the tension as you maintain that one second pause between the breaths. As you exhale, relax your fists, letting the hands and fingers completely unfold and relax. As you continue to the next inhale, again clench your fists. Pause slightly, and again as you open your hands, exhale smoothly and gently. Allow the relaxation to enter into your body. Silently say to yourself, "My hands are completely relaxed". Complete two breath cycles, breathing slowly and gently. <<pause for about 10 seconds>>

Bring your awareness to your arms. As you inhale, curl and tense the arms and fists, lifting them slightly. Hold the tension as you pause the breath. Notice this much like the muscle tension of anger. Slowly release the tension, exhale, and gently float your arms back down. Allow any negative feelings to leave your body and let the relaxation enter. Silently say to yourself, "My arms and hands are completely relaxed". Complete two breath cycles, breathing slowly and gently. <<pause for about 10 seconds>>

Bring your awareness to your shoulders. Tense the shoulders as you inhale, raising them toward your ears. With the shoulders tensed, hold the breath for just a second. As you exhale, feel the tension and negative emotions leave you. Let go of any anger. Repeat this movement again, lifting your shoulders as you tense and inhale. Hold the shoulders tensed for a moment as you hold the breath. Now exhale all tension smoothly lowering the shoulders. Let the tension drain out of your shoulders, down your arms and out your fingertips. Allow the relaxation to enter your body. Silently say to yourself, "My shoulders, arms, and hands are completely relaxed". Complete two breath cycles, breathing slowly and gently. <<pause for about 10 seconds>>

Bring your awareness to your lower legs. As you inhale, flex your feet, pointing the toes up toward you. Observe hold the tension briefly. Now exhale, allowing the feet and lower legs to relax. Notice the tension draining out of the legs. Allow any negative emotions to drain with the breath. Begin inhaling while again flexing the feet and pointing the toes. Once you have inhaled, hold the breath for a second, noticing the tension you accumulated. As you exhale, again relax the lower legs and feet. Feel the tension drain completely out of the legs. Relax and remain still, completing a couple of breath cycles. <<pause for about 10 seconds>>

Now bring your awareness to your upper legs and buttocks. Complete two breath cycles, breathing slowly and gently.

<<pause for about about 10 seconds>>

Now as you inhale, begin flexing both legs and the sitting muscles. Hold the tension after the inhale as you briefly pause the breathing. Now slowly exhale as you let go of all the tension. As you begin inhaling, again flex both legs and sitting muscles. After the inhale, pause slightly and hold. Now slowly exhale as you let go of all the tension in your legs. As you inhale, allow the relaxation to enter into your legs. Silently say to yourself, "My arms and legs are completely relaxed". Complete two breath cycles, breathing slowly and gently. <<pause for about 10 seconds>>

Bring your awareness to your face and neck. As you inhale, tense all of the muscles in your face and neck. Once you inhale, hold the breath and awareness of the tension. Begin exhaling, releasing all of the tension. Allow any leftover negative emotions to drain out of your body. Allow it all to drain out of your face, neck and body. Now inhale again, flexing your face and neck. Briefly hold the tension and the breath. Now as you exhale, release all of the tension in your neck and face. Allow the relaxation to enter your body. Silently say to yourself, "My neck, face, arms, and legs are totally relaxed". Complete two breath cycles fully relaxed, breathing slowly and gently. <<pause for about 10 seconds>>

Now continue breathing while aware of your whole body. As you inhale, moderately flex all of the muscles in your body. Briefly hold any residual tension. Now exhale, slowly letting all the muscles of your body relax. Allow any last bit of tension to drain out of your body, sinking into the earth below you. Inhale again as you lightly flex the muscles of your body. Hold the breath for just a second. Now exhale, allow total relaxation to enter into your body. Silently say to yourself, "My entire body and mind are completely relaxed".

Continue breathing as you remain comfortable. Search your body, breath, and mind for any signs of left over tension. Release any remaining pockets of tension that you may find. Notice how you feel totally relaxed. Allow that good feeling to spread through your body and settle deeply within it. Notice that your mind is at peace. Continue to breathe for a minute, enjoying the feeling of complete relaxation. <<pause for about a minute>>

Take one last deep breath. As you exhale, open your eyes, feeling refreshed and alert. Slowly and gently stretch your whole body. Feeling more alert, take another breath. Continue feeling pleasant and relaxed, getting up when it is appropriate to do so.

In both yogic breathing and yogic exercise, researchers are finding a wide range of benefits. Until recently, yoga was considered just like any other exercise. Some may say that it was just a passing fad, with approximately 1 in 10 Americans practicing yoga.[83] Now, more than any other time in history, scientific studies are being conducted regarding the benefits of yoga. Both running and swimming are considered extremely effective and beneficial forms of exercise. However, the evidence is starting to collect that almost no other form of exercise has such a wide range of benefits as yoga. Though no single study is absolutely conclusive, here is some of the scientific evidence.

Yoga has been shown to:

- Reduce hypertension, which is associated with a decrease in risk of kidney disease, stroke, and heart disease.[84]
- Help control blood sugar, cholesterol, and reduces signs of atherosclerosis.[85]
- Stimulate the vagus nerve, and contribute to overall improved immune function. [86]
- Improve the flexibility of the spine and reduce degeneration of the spine that accompanies aging.[87]
- Increase brain neurotransmitter levels in practitioners, improving mood and reducing anxiety.[88]

"I think breath is the only function through which you can influence the involuntary nervous system".-Dr. Andrew Weil[89]

Yogic breathing, of which diaphragmatic breathing is a part, has many benefits. Because there are so many ways to perform breathing exercises, no one study can conclude which exercises are best for any particular person. As such, it is highly recommended that those who wish to incorporate breathing exercises beyond the diaphragmatic breathing explained in this appendix, seek out and practice with a qualified yogic expert. Yogic breathing has been shown to:

- Impact health, behavior, and regulate moods.[90]
- Calm the mind and affect brain chemistry when performed deep and slow.[91]
- Regulate our moods, to affect how happy we are.[92]

There are many styles and modalities of yogic training. Perusing through the following resources will assist you in finding additional information:

- www.yogaalliance.org A registry of certified yoga teachers and related material.
- www.yogajournal.com The largest circulation yoga magazine.
- en.wikipedia.org An encyclopedic resource, including information on yoga.
- *Light on Pranayama* by B.K.S. Iyengar. This guide includes yogic breathing techniques from beginner to advanced.

Abbreviations

1. When we refer to a word (or words) as a trainable skill or as a specific psychological term, we capitalize those words. If we are discussing the same words, in the context of their more traditional meanings, they are not capitalized.

ACT = This stands for "Anger Control Today" and refers the instrument where participants record any anger episodes.

ICE = In-Class Exercise

OOCE = Out-of-Class Exercise

PA = Passive Aggressor

SbA = Shame-Based Anger

STS = Short-Term Strategy

LTS = Long-Term Strategy

VSS = Virtue/Strength/Skill = (Virtues, with the subcategory of Strengths, trained as skills)

Bibliography

Achor, Shawn. *Before Happiness: The 5 Hidden Keys to Achieving Success, Spreading Happiness, and Sustaining Positive Change.* New York: Crown Business, 2013.

—. *The Happiness Advantage: How a Positive Brain Fuels Success in Work and Life.* New York: Currency, 2018.

Anderson, Katie. *Meditation Techniques.* CreateSpace Independent Publishing Platform, 2015.

Anderson, Scott C., Cryan, John F., Dinan, Ted. *The Psychobiotic Revolution: Mood, Food, and the New Science of the Gut-Brain Connection.* Washington, DC: National Geographic, 2017.

Baer, Lee, Ph.D. *The Imp of the Mind: Exploring the Silent Epidemic of Obsessive Bad Thoughts.* New York: Plume, 2002.

Baum, Kenneth. *The Mental Edge.* New York: Berkley Publishing Group, 1999.

Baumgardener, Steve R., Crothers, Marie K. *Positive Psychology.* New York: Pearson, 2008.

Benson, Herbert, M.D., Klipper, Miriam Z. *The Relaxation Response.* New York: William Morrow Paperbacks, 2000.

Boza, Theresa. *Reprogram Your Brain for Happiness & Progressive Mental Health: Social Brain Healing, DNA Extraction & Strategies for Ending Rage.* Bloomington, IN: AuthorHouse, 2015.

Chapman, Gary. *Anger: Taming a Powerful Emotion.* Chicago, IL: Northfield Publishing, 2015.

Chavan, Yesenia. *Meditation for Beginners.* CreateSpace Independent Publishing Platform, 2014.

Collins, Gary R. *Christian Counseling: A Comprehensive Guide.* Nashville, TN: Thomas Nelson Inc., 2006.

Covey, Stephen R. *The 7 Habits of Highly Effective People.* New York: Simon & Schuster, 2004.

Csikszentmihalyi, Mihaly. *Finding Flow: The Psychology of Engagement with Everyday Life.* New York: Basic Books, 1998.

—. *Flow and the Foundations of Positive Psychology: The Collected Works of Mihaly Csikszentmihalyi.* New York: Springer, 2014.

—. *Flow: The Psychology of Optimal Experience.* New York: Harper Perennial Modern Classics, 2008.

Desai, Kamini. *Yoga Nidra: The Art of Transformational Sleep.* Twin Lakes, WI: Lotus Press, 2017.

Devi, Gayatri, M.D. *A Calm Brain: How to Relax into a Stress-Free, High-Powered Life*. New York: Plume, 2012.

Easterbrook, Gregg. *It's Better Than It Looks: Reasons for Optimism in an Age of Fear*. New York: PublicAffairs, 2018.

Efron-Potter, Ronald, Ph.D. *Healing the Angry Brain: How Understanding the Way Your Brain Works Can Help You Control Anger and Aggression*. Oakland, CA: New Harbinger Publications, 2012.

—. *Rage: A Step-by-Step Guide to Overcoming Explosive Anger*. Oakland, CA: New Harbinger Publications, 2007.

Efron-Potter, Ronald, Ph.D, Efron-Potter, Patricia S., M.S. *Letting Go of Anger*. Oakland, CA: New Harbinger Publications, Inc, 2006.

Ellis, Albert, Ph.D. *How to Control Your Anger Before It Controls You*. New York: Citadel Press, 2016.

Emlet, Michael R. *Descriptions and Prescriptions*. Greensboro, NC: New Growth Press, 2017.

Ford, Judy. *Getting Over Getting Mad: Positive Ways to Manage Anger in Your Most Important Relationships*. Berkeley, CA: Conari Press, 2001.

Gattuso, Joan. *The Power of Forgiveness: Forgiving as a Path to Freedom*. New York: TarcherPerigee, 2015.

Goleman, Daniel, Davidson, Richard J. *Altered Traits: Science Reveals How Meditation Changes Your Mind, Brain, and Body*. New York: Avery, 2017.

Hanh, Thich Nhat. *Happiness: Essential Mindfulness Practices*. Berkeley, CA: Parallax Press, 2005.

—. *How to Relax*. Berkeley, CA: Parallax Press, 2015.

Hanser, Suzanne B. *Manage Your Stress and Pain Through Music Book/CD*.

Harvard Business Review, Goleman, Daniel, McKee, Annie, Waytz, Adam. *Empathy (HBR Emotional Intelligence Series)*. Boston, MA: Harvard Business Review Press, 2017.

Hefferon, Kate, Boniwell, Ilona. *Positive Psychology: Theory, Research and Applications*. New York: Open University Press, 2011.

Heriza, Nirmala. *Dr. Yoga: A Complete Guide to the Medical Benefits of Yoga (Yoga for Health)*. New York: PenguinTarcher, 2004.

Hoffman, Edward, Compton, William C. *Positive Psychology 2nd Edition: The Science of Happiness and Flourishing*. Belmont, CA: Wadsworth Publishing, 2012.

Ingram, Chip, Dr. Johnson, Becca. *Overcoming Emotions That Destroy*. Grand Rapids, MI: Baker Books, 2010.

Iyengar, B.K.S. *Light on Pranayama*. London: The Crossroad Publishing Company, 1985.

Jakubowicz, Rina. *The Yoga Mind: 52 Essential Principles of Yoga Philosophy to Deepen Your Practice*. Emeryville, CA: Rockridge Press, 2018.

Jones, Robert D. *Uprooting Anger*. Phillipsburg, NJ: P & R Publishing, 2005.

Kendall, R.T. *Total Forgiveness*. Lake Mary, FL: Charisma House, 2001.

Korn, Leslie. *The Good Mood Kitchen: Simple Recipes and Nutrition Tips for Emotional Balance*. New York: W. W. Norton & Company, 2017.

Krznaric, Roman. *Empathy: Why It Matters, and How to Get It*. New York: TarcherPerigee, 2014.

Lama, Dalai. *The Art of Happiness, 10ᵗʰ Anniversary Edition: A Handbook for Living*. New York: Riverhead Books, 2009.

Levitin, Daniel. *This Is Your Brain on Music: The Science of a Human Obsession*. London: Atlantic Books, 2008.

Lopez, Shane J., Pedrotti, Teramoto, Jennifer. *Positive Psychology: The Scientific and Practical Explorations of Human Strengths*. Oaks, CA: SAGE Publications, Inc, 2014.

Lopez, Shane J., Snyder, C. R. *Oxford Handbook of Positive Psychology- 2ⁿᵈ Edition*. New York: Oxford University Press, 2011.

Lusk, Julie. *Yoga Nidra for Complete Relaxation and Stress Relief*. Oakland, CA: New Harbinger Publications, 2015.

Mayer, Emeran. *The Mind-Gut Connection: How the Hidden Conversation Within Our Bodies Impacts Our Mood, Our Choices, and Our Overall Health*. New York: Harper Wave, 2018.

McLaren, Karla. *The Art of Empathy: A Complete Guide to Life's Most Essential Skill*. Boulder, CO: Sounds True, 2013.

Meurisse, Thibaut. *Master Your Emotions: A Practical Guide to Overcome Negativity and Better Manage Your Feelings*. Amazon Digital Services LLC, 2018.

Miller, Richard. *Yoga Nidra: A Medatative Practice for Deep Relaxation and Healing*. Boulder, CO: Sounds True, 2010.

Orloff, Judith, M.D. *Emotional Freedom: Liberate Yourself from Negative Emotions and Transform Your Life*. New York: Harmony, 2009.

Ortiz, John. *The Tao of Music*. San Francisco, CA: Red Wheel/Weiser, 1997.

Ravich, Lenny. *Everlasting Optimism: 9 Principles for Success, Happiness and Powerful Relationships*. 2017.

Ricard, Matthieu. *Happiness: A Guide to Developing Life's Most Important Skill*. New York: Little, Brown and Company, 2007.

Sadhguru. *Inner Engineering: A Yogi's Guide to Joy*. New York: Spiegel & Grau, 2016.

Saraswati, Swami Satyananda. *Yoga Nidra 2009 Reprint*. Munger, India: Yoga Publications Trust, 2009.

Schiffmann, Erich, O'Rielly, Trish. *Yoga: The Spirit and Practice of Moving Into Stillness*. New York: Pocket Books, 1996.

Seligman, Martin E.P. *Authentic Happiness*. New York: Atria Books, 2004.

—. *Flourish*. New York: Atria Books, 2012.

—. *Learned Optimism: How to Change Your Mind and Your Life*. New York: Vintage, 2006.

—. *The Hope Circut*. New York: PublicAffairs, 2018.

Stanley, Issac. *Yoga: Benefits of Yoga in Day to Day life, Weight Loss, Stress Relief, Inner Peace and Ultimate Freedom*. Ténzy Publisher, 2017.

Stechkin, Sticks. *Stress Relief:Get It All Out Through Drums and Percussion*. Amazon Digital Services LLC, 2015.

Tafrate, Raymond Chip, Ph.D, Kassinove, Howard, Ph.D. *Anger Management for Everyone: Seven Proven Ways to Control Anger and Live a Happier Life*. Oakland, CA: Impact, 2009.

Tipping, Colin. *Radical Forgiveness: A Revolutionary Five-Stage Process to Heal Relationships, Let Go of Anger and Blame, and Find Peace in Any Situation*. Boulder, CO: Sounds True, 2010.

Tolle, Eckhart. *The Power of Now*. Novato, CA: New World Library, 2010.

Tutu, Desmond. *The Book of Forgiving: The Fourfold Path for Healing Ourselves and Our World*. New York: HarperOne, 2014.

Wallace, Ruth-Leyse. *Nutrition and Mental Health*. Boca Raton, FL: CRC Press, 2013.

Walsh, William J. *Nutrient Power: Heal Your Biochemistry and Heal Your Brain*. New York: Skyhorse Publishing, 2014.

Wheeler, Barbara L. *Music Therapy Research*. New Braunfels, TX: Barcelona Publishers, 2016.

Winner, Jay, M.D. *Relaxation on the Run: Simple Methods to Reduce Stress in Seconds Plus Practical Lifestyle Tips for a Happier and Healthier Life*. Santa Barbara, CA: Blue Fountain Press, 2015.

https://positivepsychologyprogram.com/category/optimism/

This site has information on positive psychology, and specifically regarding optimism

www.yogaalliance.org

This site has yoga related information, including an extensive registry of registered yoga teachers.

Gillihan, Seth J., Ph.D. *7 Ways Yoga Lowers Stress and Anxiety*. 15 September 2016. https://www.psychologytoday.com/us/blog/think-act-be/201609/7-ways-yoga-lowers-stress-and-anxiety

Golden, Bernard, Ph.D. *When Anger Management Requires Going Deeper*. 29 January 2018. https://www.psychologytoday.com/us/blog/overcoming-destructive-anger/201801/when-anger-management-requires-going-deeper

Joaquín. *Understanding Empathy: What is it and Why is it Important in Counseling*. 8 August 2017. https://positivepsychologyprogram.com/empathy

Learned Optimism: The Cup Half Full. 22 September 2016. https://positivepsychologyprogram. com/learned-optimism/

O'Grady, Patty, Ph.D,. *The Positive Psychology of Empathy.* 14 March 2013. https://www. psychologytoday.com/us/blog/positive-psychology-in-the-classroom/201303/ the-positive-psychology-empathy.

Radford, Nancy. *Forgiveness: The Key To a Happier Future.* 11 April 2016. https:// positivepsychologyprogram.com/forgiveness/.

Selhub, Eva, M.D. *Nutritional Psychiatry: Your Brain on Food.* 16 November 2015. https://www. health.harvard.edu/blog/nutritional-psychiatry-your-brain-on-food-201511168626.

Taibbi, Robert, L.C.S.W. *3 Keys to Anger Management.* 16 April 2014. https://www. psychologytoday.com/us/blog/fixing-families/201404/3-keys-anger-management.

Turner, Doug. *THE MIRACLE AND THE IRONY OF FORGIVING.* 15 June 2007. https:// positivepsychologynews.com/news/doug-turner/20070615298.

Wei, Marlynn, M.D., J.D. *Yoga for Stress Relief.* 8 December 2015. https://www.psychologytoday. com/us/blog/urban-survival/201512/yoga-stress-relief.

Endnotes

Introduction:

1   National Geographic Video, Stress : Portrait of a Killer (2008), featuring Dr. Robert Sapolsky

Chapter 1:

2   en.wikipedia.org/wiki'/Positive_Psychology
3   Ibid
4   psychology.about.com/od/branchesofpsychology1/a/positive-psychology.htm
5   hubpages.com/education/The-Most-Popular-Class-at-Harvard-University-Positive-Psychology-The-Science-of-Happiness
6   Martin E.P. Seligman, PhD, Authentic Happiness, Simon & Schuster : New York, (2002), pgs 45-121
7   Ibid, pg 47
8   Ibid, pg 61
9   http://psychology.about.com/od/PositivePsychology/a/flow.htm
10   Martin E.P. Seligman, PhD, Authentic Happiness, Simon & Schuster : New York, (2002), pgs 132-133
11   Staw, B., R., and Pelled, L (1994) Employee positive emotion and favorable outcomes at the workplace, Organization Science, (5) 51-71
12   Martin E.P. Seligman, PhD, Authentic Happiness, Simon & Schuster : New York, (2002), pg 43
13   greatergood.berkeley.edu/topic/forgiveness/definition

Chapter 2:

14   SuperSize Me, DVD, Kathbur Pictures Inc. (2004) and Harp Sharp Video : New York, (2004)

Chapter 3:

15   Martin E.P. Seligman, PhD, Authentic Happiness, Simon & Schuster : New York, (2002), pg 47
16   Berkowitz 1970; Murray 1985; Straus, Gelles, & Steinmetz 1990
17   Tarasoff v. Regents of the University of California, 529 P. 2d 553, Cal. 1974
18   Ronald T. Potter-Efron, MSW, PhD and Patricia S. Potter-Efron, MS, Letting Go of Anger, Oakland, CA : New Harbinger Publications, Inc., (2006)

19   Rabbi Moshe Weiner, The Divine Code, second edition, Ask Noah International (2011), pg 121

20   Gil Fronsdal, "The Dhammapada : A New Translation of the Buddhist Classic with Annotations", Shambhala Books : Boston, (2005), pgs 51-61

Chapter 4:

21   time.com/3972327/teen-poem-bar-brooklyn/

22   Stephen R. Covey, The 7 Habits of Highly Effective People, Simon & Schuster : New York, (2004), pgs 215-246

Chapter 5:

23   Martin E.P. Seligman, PhD, Authentic Happiness, Simon & Schuster : New York, (2002), pg 120

Chapter 6:

<none>

Chapter 7:

24   https://draxe.com/limbic-system/

Chapter 8:

<none>

Chapter 9:

25   Efron et. al., Letting Go of Anger, Oakland, CA : New Harbinger Publications, Inc., (2006), pg 100

26   Edwin F. Bryant, The Yoga Sutras of Patanjali, New York : North Point Press (2009) pgs 488-489

Chapter 10:

<none>

Chapter 11:

<none>

Chapter 12:

27 Witvliet, C.V., Ludwig, T.E., & Vander Laan, K.L., Psychological Sciences, (2001), pgs 117-123

28 Martin E.P. Seligman, PhD, Authentic Happiness, Simon & Schuster : New York, (2002), pg 81

29 www.pursuit-of-happiness.org/history-of-happiness/martin-seligman-psychology/

Chapter 13:

<none>

Chapter 14:

<none>

Appendix M (Music Therapy):

30 The Secret Teachings of the Ages, Manly P. Hall, Wilder Publications (2007), pg 219

31 www.cerebromente.org.br/n15/mente/musica.html

32 www.dovesong.com/positive_music/plant_experiments.asp

33 International Journal of Environmental Science and Development, Vol. 5, No. 5, October 2014, pgs 431-434

34 C. Hicks, "Growing Corn to Music", Popular Mechanics, 183, May 1963, pgs 118-121

35 www.highexistence.com/water-experiment/

36 Plethora of articles. Search: Bioelectromagnetics; "Calcite microcrystals in the pineal gland"; "Magnetite biomineralization in the human brain"; or "magnetic and high-resolution transmission electron microscopy".

37 www.cerebromente.org.br/n15/mente/musica.html

38 Ibid

39 Ibid

40 Ibid

41 Ibid citing Dr. Leslie A. Chambers and Dr. Earl W. Flosdorf

42 www.wsj.com/articles/army-test-hearing-drug-at-the-rifle-range-1440182197 (accessed January 21, 2016)

43 serendip.brynmawr.edu/exchange/node/2486

44 https://www.ncbi.nlm.nih.gov Read: "Extreme Metal Music and Anger Processing"

45 Ibid

46 Anderson, C.A., Carnagey, N.L., Eubanks, J. (2003), Exposure to violent media: The effects of songs with violent lyrics and aggressive thoughts and feelings. Journal of Personality and Social Psychology, 84, 960-971

47 www.babycenter/com/404_is-listening-to-negative-lyrics-or-angry-music-really-harmful-for-my-child?

48 Ibid

49 www.cnn.com/2013/04/15/health/brain-music-research/

50 Ibid

51 psychcentral.com/lib/the-power-of-music-to-reduce-stress

52 www.cerebromente.org.br/n15/mente/musica.html

53 Ibid

54 Ibid

55 Ibid

56 www.cnn.com/2013/04/15/health/train-music-research/

57 www.cerebromente.org.br/n15/mente/musica.html

58 Lai, H. L., Chen, C. J., Peng, T. C., Chang, F. M., Hsieh, M. L., Huang, H. Y., Change, S. C. (2006). Randomized controlled trial of music during kangaroo (a style of care in the study) care on the maternal state and anxiety and preterm infants' responses. International Journal of Nursing Studies, 43, pgs 139-46

59 www.heart-soul-music.com/subpages/calmingeffects.html

60 holisticonline.com/stress/stress_music-therapy.htm

61 www.urbandharma.org/udharma8/monkstudy.html

62 www.ncbi.nlm.nih.gov/pmc/articles/PMC3957486/ (by EA Miendlarzewska - 2013)

63 archive.seacoastonline.com/2003/news/12292003news/d.htm

64 psychcentral.com/lib/the-power-of-music-to-reduce-stress/2/

65 Christopher Rea, Pamelyn MacDonald, Gwen Carnes, Listening to classical, pop, and metal music: An investigation of mood, Emporia State Research Studies,(2010) Vol. 46, no.1, pgs 1-3

66 Ibid

67 holisticonline.com/stress/stress_music-therapy.htm

Appendix N (Nutrition):

68 www.naturalnews.com/038322_DSM-5_psychiatry/false_diagnosis.html

69 Don Colbert, MD, The New Bible Cure for Depression and Anxiety, published by Siloam (2004), pg 53

70 drhoffman.com/wp-content/plugins/post2pdf-converter/post2

71 Ibid

72 ajcn.nutrition.org/content/86/5/1470.full

73 Don Colbert, MD, The New Bible Cure for Depression and Anxiety, published by Siloam (2004), pg 53

Appendix P (Power of Thoughts and Words):

74 Kenneth Baum, The Mental Edge, Berkley Publishing Group : NY, (1999), pg 74

75 Ibid, pg 26

76 Ibid, pg 27

77 Ibid

78 Ibid, pg 28

79 www.thecommonsenseshow.com/2016/05/27/this-is-our-best-weapon-to-fight-tyranny

80 http://noosphere.princeton.edu/

Appendix S (Spiritual/Morals Therapy)

81   Martin E.P. Seligman, PhD, Authentic Happiness, Simon & Schuster : New York (2002), pgs 132-133

82   www.dailymail.co.uk/news/article-1275574/Babies-know-difference-good-evil-months-study-reveals.html

Appendix Y

83   Yoga Alliance, http://www.prenewswire.com/news-releases/2016-yoga-in-america-study-conducted-by-yoga-journal-and-yoga-alliance-reveals-growth-and-benefits-of-the-practice-300203418.html

84   Debbie L. Cohen, LeAnne T. Bloedon, Rand L. Rothman, "Iyengar Yoga versus Enhanced Usual Care on Blood Pressure in Patients with Prehypertension State I Hypertension. A Randomized Controlled Trial", eCAM, Oxford University Press, September 4, (2009), pg 1-8

85   Kim E. Innes, Cheryl Bourguignon, and Ann Gill Taylor, "Risk Indices Associated with the Insulin Resistance Syndrome, Cardiovascular Disease, and Possible Protection with Yoga: A Systematic Review", Journal of American Board of Family Medicine, vol. 18, no. 6, November-December 2005, pgs 491-519

86   Kevin J. Tracey, "The Inflammatory Reflex", Nature, vol. 420, no. 6917, December 19-26, 2002, pgs 853-859

87   Chin-Ming Jeng, Tzu-Chieh Cheng, Ching-Huei Kung, et. al., "Yoga and Disc Degenerative Disease in Cervical and Lumbar Spine: An MR Imaging-based Case Control Study", European Spine Journal, vol. 20, no. 3, March 2011, pgs 408-413

88   Chris C. Streeter, Theodore H. Whitfield, Liz Owen, et. al., "Effects of Yoga Versus Walking on Mood, Anxiety, and Brain GABA Levels : A Randomized Controlled MRS Study", Journal of Alternative and Complementary Medicine, vol. 16, no. 11, 2010, pgs 1145-52

89   Time Magazine, November 16, 2015, pg 30

90   Kovoor T. Behanan, "Yoga: A Scientific Evaluation, New York : MacMillam, (1937), pg 243

91   Richard P. Brown and Patricia L. Gerbarg, Sudarshan Kriya Yogic Breathing in the Treatment of Stress, Anxiety, and Depression : Part 1 - Neurophysiologic Model, Journal of Alternative and Complementary Medicine, vol. 11, no. 1, 2005, pgs 189-201

92   Robert E. Thayer, "The Origin of Everyday Moods", New York : Oxford University Press (1996)

About the Authors

MARC "SATTVA" NOBLITT, Ph.D., a prodigy from the age of seven, is one of the most prominent and sought after yoga masters in the world. He has spent his life travelling the globe, seeking, studying, and training under some of the world's greatest yoga masters, martial arts masters, academic experts, and ancient Chinese medical masters. As an internationally recognized yoga master he has integrated ancient, holistic and all-natural practices with modern anti-aging technologies while benefiting thousands of students over the past four decades.

JEFFREY CHARLES BRUTEYN, Ph.D., is a former investment banking executive and CEO of two publically traded investment companies. Through a series of life changing events, he became interested in counseling and helping others. He earned a master's degree and Ph.D. in psychology and Christian counseling. He is also the author of Suicidal Kings: The Road to Redemption and Prisoner to Profiteer: How to Become a Millionaire Within Ten Years, with a focus on financial counseling. He has spent the past twelve years working with anger management, specializing in group therapy coordination.

Printed in the United States
By Bookmasters